Yabbadabbadoo

Yabbadabbadoo

JOAN BELK

ISIS
LARGE PRINT
Oxford

First published in Great Britain 2004
by
Bound Biographies Limited

Published in Large Print 2006 by ISIS Publishing Ltd.,
7 Centremead, Osney Mead, Oxford OX2 0ES
by arrangement with the author c/o
Bound Biographies Limited

British Library Cataloguing in Publication Data
Belk, Joan
  Yabbadabadoo. – Large print ed.
  (Isis reminiscence series)
  1. Belk, Joan
  2. Large type books
  3. Women – Great Britain – Biography
  4. Great Britain – Social life and customs – 20th
  century
  I. Title
  941'.082'092

ISBN 0–7531–9356–6 (hb)
ISBN 0–7531–9357–4 (pb)
ISBN 978–0–7531–9357–0 (pb)

Printed and bound in Great Britain by
T. J. International Ltd., Padstow, Cornwall

To the memories of the two men in my life,
Dad and Albert;
They sadly never met on this earth . . . but who knows?

Contents

Acknowledgements

To my daughter Pauline, son-in-law Tony, and grandson Mark; my brother John and sister-in-law Floss; my sister-in-law Doris, my good friend Doreen, and neighbours and friends, especially Pat and Jean. Thank you all for being such good friends. Thanks also to Mike for being a gentle bully in guiding me through this project. It's been great fun.

Childhood

I was born on 5th December 1924 in Tusmore Street, Rotherham, the second child of Jesse Nicholas and Ethel May Overton (nee Seddons). My brother, Ernest, was six years my senior, and my two younger brothers, John, Jesse and Peter, were also born at six-year intervals so there was a span of 24 years between us.

It was only a terraced house, but Dad turned the front room into a shop — they did have small corner shops in those days. (Even though ours was not on a corner, it was still known as a corner shop!) It sold general groceries, ice cream and sweets. Mum made the ice cream in a hand-turned churn, like a butter churn, which took a good while to do as there was no electricity in those days — can you imagine it? Word got around that my mum's ice cream was beautiful, so they came from other small shops to see if she would make some for them to sell, and she did, even though it was hard work. The secret was using Carnation evaporated milk. She knew a thing or two, my mum did.

When I was between three and four years old I contracted meningitis, or inflammation of the brain. It was touch and go, but they didn't even send me to hospital. There was an epidemic and there were about six of us in town, one of whom was my future sister-in-law who became a slow mover and a slow talker. At about midnight Doctor Agnew was called, and he said that there was no chance that I would live — he was very sorry, but that was that.

Dad wasn't having any of this. There were no buses because the last one had gone, and there were no taxis and we didn't have a car, so he set off walking about five miles out of town to a small village called Treeton. There was a herbalist living there that Dad knew, a Mr Walton, who had a herb stall in the market. He came back with Dad and knocked up Mr Limb, the chemist who lived over the shop. Mr Walton told my dad to ask for some mistletoe powder, which is a poison. The chemist supplied this, asking Dad if it was for meningitis. Dad probably had to sign for it. Mr Walton told Dad to give me one spot at a time, to wrap me up in old pieces of sheet down below, and wait. He warned that the smell would be atrocious. Mum and Dad didn't have a dropper, so Dad used a feather. He had to watch that he didn't give me more than one drop at a time, and then they sat back and waited for the "crisis" — if I got through this I would survive.

I remember feeling as though I was falling through the bed, and all I could say was "Mum, Mum," and then I fell unconscious. Then it happened — the poison had moved down my spine, and I had something like an abscess on my neck which burst and oozed horrible stuff. Then the poison travelled down and came out down below, and Mum said that the stench was

2

overpowering. My Auntie Lily and Uncle Frank from next door came in to give them a hand. The neighbours had already given them pieces of old sheeting — neighbours used to help in those days. They brought newspapers to wrap the sheets up in and put them in the bin, ready to burn the next morning. This went on through the night until Mum washed me down and I fell into a deep sleep.

The next day the doctor came — he was pleased that I had got over the crisis, but they had to see what I was like when I woke up, because I could have been left with all sorts of things — brain damage etc. My dad didn't tell the doctor about Mr Walton because he didn't know how they stood, as I believe the Witchcraft Act was still in force and Mr Walton and the chemist could have been prosecuted. Anyway, it came to dinnertime, and all of a sudden I woke up, sat up, and said, "Mum, I want some of Doris's pie."

"Right, love," she said, "You'll have some." So she went to Doris's cafe, the back of which was in our yard. The door was always open and I could smell the meat and potato pie, which Doris was well known for. Mum brought some on a dish with some nice gravy on it, and I ate a bit of it with a spoon. Then I closed my eyes and went back to sleep — I was lucky. Dad went to see Mr Walton to tell him what had happened, and to pay him, but Mr Walton wouldn't take anything. He said that he got his reward by knowing that I was alive and that I was all right, not being left with any brain damage. I was very lucky, as meningitis can be a killer.

About twelve months later Dad managed to rent a colliery house in Brinsworth, a village just outside Rotherham, in the country. Brinsworth had one pub, the *Atlas Hotel*, one church and churchyard, about three farms and two schools, the junior and senior. The two long streets were Ellis Street and Duncan Street. Our houses were colliery houses, though there weren't many miners. Those who didn't work down the pit worked for either Steel, Peech and Tozers, one of the biggest steelworks in the world, or on the railway. I couldn't understand why half of the houses were owned by the colliery and the other half by the railway. The railway along the top of our street was for steam engines — probably coal and railways were combined in Victorian days, about when the houses were built.

Dad was honest and a disciplinarian. I think I must take after him because as a child I was a bookworm, studying anything interesting, learning what I could (and I still do). The only thing that was wrong with me was that I was terribly shy, quiet and docile. In later years this was to change.

Dad had started work as a miner at the age of 13, and here in Brinsworth he had a pit pony called Mark. Dad looked after him, and always took Mark bread and jam, of which he was very fond, and also carrots and apples. Dad said that if you looked after your pony he would work well for you.

I was an inquisitive child and used to ask Dad all sorts of questions. For example, how did he get down the pit? Answer — by a large lift that took them to the bottom, and then sometimes they had a ride in wagons which took them a couple of miles, but sometimes they had to walk. The ground was wet and the ceiling low, so Dad had to work on his hands and knees using his pick and shovel — it must have been agony. He was caught in a fall of coal once and had to be dug out. He was lucky that he wasn't hurt too much, but he had blue scars on his body, which was coal dust that had got caught in the wounds. I remember hearing an explosion one day, and we went to the pithead, but it wasn't too serious and the men were rescued, thank goodness.

One day at school we were being taught about the uses of coal, so the teacher marched us down to the pit and they took us round the plant to see what was extracted from coal. This was very interesting — they made tar, sulphur, benzoline, disinfectant, and many other products. When these had been extracted only the coke was left, which Dad brought home for a nominal fee of 1/-, for which he could take as much as he wanted. So he used to sit me on the barrow going down, but I would have to walk back. We would go several times in one day.

He also did the same again when buying railway sleepers, tar, tarred railings, and anything that was going. Dad was very enterprising, you see, and I remember him saying to me, "You can make anything out of next to nothing, Pidge (short for little pigeon). Are you taking notice? you might need this knowledge." I did need it in later years, and it stood me in good stead as I put it into practice when I was practically destitute.

Dad also made hair cream, hair-setting lotion and hair tonic. The hair lotion was tried out on me one day, and my hair went as stiff as a board. "Oh, I've put too much gum arabic in," Dad said. So he tried again and got it right. Mind you, it soon washed out of my hair, so everything was all right.

My father also made furniture polish with beeswax, which used to bring up a right shine on furniture. Another thing that he did was to sell sweets down the pit — you see, miners couldn't smoke because of the potentially lethal gases, so they chewed most of the time, usually twist (raw tobacco). He used to have toffees delivered by the hundredweight, and Mum and I would count them out into bags, 2d and 4d per quarter depending on the brand — Bluebird Toffees, Dainty Dinah and Radiance, all best quality. He always took them in a black apron Mum had made into a pouch and which he tied around his waist. He stood on Fridays near the pay office with his red book and collected his money. Nobody missed payment as Dad was on the spot, so they had no excuse for not paying. I often wondered where Dad got his ideas from — now I know where I get my ideas.

In the meantime Mum made ointment and cough mixture — there's no wonder we hardly ever went to the doctor's, what with organic vegetables, fresh air, and having plenty of energy running about and playing games. Mum was very busy in the summer, making bottles and bottles of nettle ginger ale which were sold to the miners when they came up from the pit at 2d per bottle.

Mum had started in the Lancashire textile mills, also from the age of 13, after she ran away from home with her younger brother Ernest (Ern) and sister Doris. She had two other younger sisters, but they both died in infancy. Her dad had died when he was only 29, having developed galloping consumption from his work as a glass-blower. After a while, her mother married again, as she had been left with five children. Their stepfather, a man named Booker, wasn't very good to them; in fact he was mean, doling out a slice-and-a-half of bread to them per meal. Mum managed to rent a small terraced house near the mills at two shillings and sixpence per week. Her younger sister Doris worked half a day and went to school the other half Ern worked as a lather boy for a barber, and so that's how they managed — that's what I call survival.

Number 104 Ellis Street, where we lived, was a three-bedroom terraced house with a toilet at the bottom of the garden. There were two large bedrooms and a smaller one, a large kitchen, a front room, and a pantry. We loved the house; it was only 15 minutes walk away from the pit where Dad worked and the schools were nearby on the doorstep. There was no hot water in the house, and only gaslight. I remember when the colliery decided to put electricity in — it was magic! We kept switching it on and off until Mum threatened us with violence, and so then we stopped.

Our house was a decent size, with a large kitchen, which had an iron fireplace with a largish oven and coal fire. The sink was a horrible stone one for a few years, and we had a brass cold-water tap and an enamel washing-up bowl. Every Monday was the marathon of washday. As soon as the children were sent to school, Mum would start the washing, putting it into piles: whites (towels, sheets, pillow slips), darks and woollen items. Some hot water was put aside for Dad's pit clothes which were kept separate because of the coal dust. We had a copper between the sink and the fireplace, and it had a lid on top of it when not in use. On the other side of the fireplace was a long narrow boiler, which was topped up with an enamel ladling can.

Mum started up the coal fire under the copper, and when the water was hot she would empty it into the wash-tub, and refill the copper with cold water. With soap powder, Rinso and soda in the tub, the whites would be done first. Mum would get the ponch, which was shaped like a thick basin copper with holes in it (like an upturned colander) and a brush stale (broom handle) fastened to it. She would ponch them up and down for about 20 minutes, then use the rubbing board to rub them, using Fairy soap, and then ring the clothes out and put them in a bath of cold water. The whole procedure would then be repeated again, and at the end they would be put in a bath of cold water with Dolly Blue to whiten them up.

My mother would hang out the washing to dry, and start again. If it was raining she would hang them in the house from the ceiling on a large rack that Dad had put up. This was a contraption that held about five long rods and was raised or lowered with a rope tied to a large hook on the wall. It was very handy and dried sheets overnight.

Some items like shirt collars needed starching, so these were immersed in a solution of Robin starch. When we came home from school on a Monday the copper had cold water added to cool it down and we'd sit on the sides with our feet dangling in. When Mum wanted to wash us, we'd stand up. Sometimes it was still hot at the bottom and we would dance up and down while Mum told us to be still. After bathing us in the water left in the copper, Mum would empty it out and scrub the outside toilet seat, windowsill and steps, and finish off by scrubbing the grate by the outside drain — boy, that water went a long way, and you didn't waste anything!

Mum then served us dinner as we sat around the table — we were not allowed to eat with food on our knees. We used to have cold meat, bubble and squeak (potato, cabbage and peas all fried together), pickled onions or red cabbage, bread and butter and an enamel mug of tea. We had this every washday.

In our pantry we had a long marble table which was very cold and we always had a plentiful supply of pickled onions, red cabbage, a large chunk of cheese, cucumber and onions sliced in vinegar, a pot of pork dripping and a row of oven bottom cakes, which were all cheap to make.

On Tuesday Mum would iron everything with two flat irons. This took some time as they had to be heated on the fire, which had to be glowing rather than smoking. There was a little shelf that hung in front of the grate. Mum would rub the iron with a piece of soap to make it run smoothly, then on a cloth to keep it clean. The clothes would be hung on the rack to air.

On Wednesday Mum cleaned upstairs, scrubbing the floors after making the beds, putting the clean washing away, and cooking our meals and baking the bread, all done in the oven at the side of the fireplace. She would clean all the windows and scrub the kitchen floor (tiled red with navy diamond shaped tiles) until it shone. It was all scrub in those days.

We pegged rag rugs for the hearth from old coats we had finished with — Mum would take them to pieces, wash them, cut them into clippings, and peg them into a piece of hessian with half a peg. I was still doing this when my husband deserted us in 1959, because we were practically penniless and had to survive somehow. I never had a vacuum cleaner, washing machine or gas cooker, so I was doing exactly the same as Mum had done years before well into the 1960s.

At the back of our house was a spare piece of land and across this was Dad's allotment, rather a large one. One end was a small chicken farm, where we had ducks and geese. I knew the names of all the types of hens — White Leghorns, Rhode Island Reds, etc. We also had a beautiful big cockerel strutting about with a red comb on his head — we called him "Thing". Dad had bought an old tram, sawn it in half, put a new roof on it, taken the windows out and put shutters up. He put a shelf round with nesting boxes underneath, and the hens were ecstatic, flitting in and out all day. I used to collect the eggs every day with a basket, and we also had duck eggs. The geese were a different kettle of fish. They were guarding the place against people, cats and foxes.

We had Bantam hens at home in the back garden, and they all had names — Hetty, Betty, Bertha, Clara and Mary etc. After a meal Mum used to call them into the house and they'd clear all the crumbs up, as good as any vacuum cleaner, which we didn't have in those days of course. The fireplace had to be either black-leaded or polished every day until you could see your face in it, and then all the ashes and clinkers from under the oven had to be taken to the bottom of the garden. These were used in winter on slippery paths. Eggshells weren't wasted either, and they were crushed and used as grit for the birds.

At the bottom of our side of Ellis Street was a large Victorian building which housed two shops — a grocer's and a pork shop. As we were at the bottom of the street, they were only a few doors down. Opposite us was a yard that belonged to the back of four shops, in which there was an abattoir where pigs were killed for the pork shop. The strange thing was that it was only about 70 yards from our house, and as children we didn't think anything of it. We never took any notice, and soon even got used to the horrendous squeal of the poor condemned pigs being strung up by their legs awaiting their fate.

We had a happy enough childhood, although Mum and Dad were opposites and never agreed about anything. Dad was a bit of an eccentric — I love eccentrics, they are different and have so much character. He studied law books, and anyone who

11

needed a solicitor used to come to Dad so that he could go to court with them. I remember him coming home once after one of these excursions. He and his mates had been to an auction to buy their allotments as they had come up for sale. Dad was supposed to be bidding for them, but one of his own side bid against him, which made the price go up. He called him "Lard Head" and shouted that he hadn't got the brains of a gnat, and a few other choice phrases. I couldn't stop laughing, and Dad saw the funny side of it after a while . . . how we did laugh!

My Dad was a philosopher. "Now, take Mr Micawber, for instance," he would say. "Say you have a pound, spend nineteen shillings and sixpence and you are all right; spend one pound and sixpence and you are in debt and in trouble." Another one: "Always pay your rent first, at least you've got a roof over your head." And yet another: "Listen to yourself and your instinct, don't let anyone dangle a carrot in your face — weigh things up before you accept anything." These I act on to this day; he had many more sayings and anecdotes.

Mum was a good mother. As I've already said, we hardly ever went to the doctor's as she made her own ointments and cough mixture. If we had a cold she'd make a little cotton bag and put a piece of camphor ice (little transparent squares) in it, then hang it round our necks, and the cold would soon disappear.

A strange thing happened with Mum. Up until the age of 39 she was shy, like me, but when the war broke out she went to work in a big steel works as a crane driver, and that brought her out of her shell and she became a right character. In later years, my dear husband, Albert, used to say, "Your Mum has charisma, Joan; everyone likes her." She was very witty and we both shared the same sense of humour.

Mum would lime-wash out the place where we used to put the rubbish bins to get rid of spiders and insects living there. She used this place as a hairdressing "salon", 1d for the children, 2d for the men. When we went back to school after the summer holidays she would have a queue waiting — girls for a trim, boys for short back and sides. They looked like clones when she had finished, but this was done to prevent lice, and as there was no medication available, Mum would rub paraffin into the hair, leave it for a minute or two, then wash it with warm vinegar — that got rid of them! I used the same treatment when I washed my hair when I was in the Air Force, and I had no trouble.

Our old tin bath hung in the bin hole, and was brought out on Sunday night for us to have a bath before school on Monday. While Mum bathed the boys, I had to sit with my back towards them, so that I didn't see anything. So I used to read. Dad had probably gone to the pub, and I had to wait until everyone went to bed before I could have my bath. I enjoyed this as I loved baths.

One night when I was in the bath, out came a big cockroach (or blackclock as we called them) — I threw a shoe at it and it scuttled under the copper.

I told Dad next day, and he got out the creosote and cement to bung up any little hole he could find. That stopped them. Because our houses were colliery-owned, the foundations were ashes from the pits, and cockroaches loved this. They would breed happily if you didn't stop them. There were never any upstairs, but when we came downstairs in the morning and were about to put anything on to wear, we would shake it out just in case! Even to this day I shake my clothes before I put them on, and I don't think I'll ever get out of this habit. The insects were horrible, and rather large.

We played out all day when we were children; being in the fresh air we were always hungry and so we often went in and made a sandwich or got a banana — a hand of bananas cost a shilling and you could get 13 oranges for the same price, so we could always have a banana or orange whenever we wanted. However, there were no sweets for us — we didn't have money to waste on them, and there were no overweight children, not least because we were all very active. We walked, ran or cycled everywhere as cars were unheard of, except for the very rich — there were certainly none in our street.

Along the bottom of our street was the lane that led up to three farms and a white cottage where the milkman lived. He had a horse and cart, and the horse was so used to the round that it went from place to place on its own, stopping outside each house. We had hawkers come round — these were people who sold fruit, fish and rabbits from a horse and cart. The pot man sold pots and pans from a lorry that he had built a frame on to, and there was a man who sold pikelets, oatcakes and muffins. The paper lad sold *The Star*, although he was not a "lad", but a 23-year-old man who shouted "Star", and his mum doted on him, saying, "They won't fetch my lad up, because he has a dicky heart" However, he was called up, and he survived the fighting in the desert at EI Alamein. When he came home we didn't recognize him, as he walked with his back straight and his head up — it just shows you what the Army did for people. There was also a coalman, and a lamplighter for the gas lights. These lights were handy for swinging on — we used ropes from around the orange boxes bought from the fruit shop for 1d each ... but I always seemed to hit my head on the lamp so I gave it up as a bad job.

Coming back down the lane was a cottage that belonged to the caretaker of the school. The school itself was a large imposing Victorian building, well, really two, as there was the junior and senior school. We all went there, and though they were elementary schools they were excellent, and all four of us had a good education.

I was in the school choir, and one day, as we were singing *Nymphs and Shepherds*, Digger our dog came through the door with his chain trailing behind — he had broken free from his kennel, and when he saw me he dashed towards me with his tail wagging. He went under the chair on which Miss Davis was conducting, with her baton raised, knocking her over in the process. Down she came, and oh, was I in for it! She pushed her glasses up her nose.

"Joan Ovaltine (my name was Overton, so why she always called me that, I don't know, and I wasn't going to try to put her straight). Tell your father to fasten him up more securely, and take him home at once."

I dragged Digger home, and said to Mum, "The dog's got loose again, he's caused Miss Davis to have an accident"

"Oh dear, is she hurt?"

"No, Mum," I replied, "she was put out though."

I was trying to be posh — it was my age; I was a teenager, as they call them now. Of course, such terms were not used then. I was a "maid's size" if Mum took me for any clothes. I hated that term; it reminded me of mediaeval times. I would have loved to have been called a teenager, but the term was unheard of.

Peter was in the church choir some years later, and as he was getting ready to leave in his beautiful white surplice, John came up behind him and slapped him on the back. The only problem was that John had been fixing his bike and his hands were covered in oil . . . and so was the surplice now, bearing the mark of a large handprint. Peter was gloriously unaware of this . . . until he got to church when his friends were only too willing to draw it to his attention. As we received 3d for being in the choir, Peter made sure that the Vicar never saw his back as he didn't want to forego this pocket money.

I was athletic at school, playing rounders, netball, etc. I was also head girl, so one of my duties was to book latecomers, stand and look at their hands, and see if they had clean necks and shoes. My brother John used to get up my nose by wearing a small scarf that belonged to my mother, as a cravat, so we called him

"Gentleman John". I could never see if his neck had been washed, but you could never part him from that scarf — he was so obstinate at times!

It was a complete surprise to me when I was appointed head girl, as I followed a head girl who had beautiful dark curly hair and a good personality. I was shy, with straight blonde hair, and I thought I was plain. Of course that was being self-conscious. My three brothers and myself were all intelligent but we couldn't go to high school or grammar school because we were poor and couldn't afford the uniform.

Now, still coming back down the lane, was the fish and chip shop. It was an immaculate place, and Mrs Bennet owned it. She was a lovely lady, and very polite. Every time she served us she asked if we wanted "scraps" (the crispy bits of batter from the fish). Of course, our answer was always "Oh, yes, please" because it made the chips go twice as far. Her daughter was not allowed to play with us as they were middle class, owning several fish and chip shops in the area. Audrey Bennet went to a different school and was learning to play the violin, or strangling it anyway — we preferred the noise of the squealing pigs! I wondered if she should have learnt to play something else, like a saxophone — I still love saxophones.

The recreation ground was next to the fish and chip shop with a lovely stone wall adjoining. We all used to sit on this — boys and girls, as we were a mixed school — and talk and laugh for hours. One day Mr Williams walked by and someone shouted, "Slogger". He was the Welsh games teacher and had been a rugby player in his youth. We were at assembly next morning when he stood up and said in a loud voice, "Come forward the one who shouted 'Slogger' yesterday as they sat on the wall." Nobody moved. He called all our names out, and we all went up to the front "I will find out the one who said it — all hold your hands out." He hesitated to wait if anyone owned up, but they didn't, and we all got the cane . . . but nobody dared utter that name again. None of us cried, although it was not easy to keep the tears back.

One day our Pete rushed up to me to tell me that John had gone down the manhole in the recreation ground — we always called it a manhole, but it was a very large pipe that went about half a mile underground up the lane to the fishpond. It was probably an overflow pipe. Anyway, I went for Mum, and she ventured up the pipe after John. She kept calling his name, but he wasn't having any of it. " I am not coming out," he kept shouting, so she crept further up, listening to his voice, and then she grabbed him. Boy, did he cop it — he smelt terrible so she waltzed him up the road, got the bath out and gave him a rough wash, by the sound of it! Then she made him go to bed — he didn't do that again in a hurry.

The end of the lane met the main road to Rotherham, and here was a large Victorian hotel, the *Atlas*. Mr Leary was the landlord, a small grizzled Irishman who didn't like kids. He always looked old to us, he never smiled, and he shooed us away every time he saw us. The only time he couldn't was when the Doncaster races were on. We children all used to congregate around the pub for when the race-goers came back from the races in the charabancs. They used to throw us packets of butterscotch and Pontefract cakes made of liquorice, which we loved.

Across the road was the bottom field with the horses in, and adjacent to that was St George's, the church, and churchyard with the cenotaph. Then the allotments were next, and then four shops —m Walton's bread and pastry shop, the butcher's shop, Cockin's fruit shop, and finally Black's grocery shop. These were all on the front of the yard with the abattoir — so we are back to square one, the bottom of our street.

My brother John was the butcher boy. He always wore a cowboy suit with chaps and bells dangling from the bottom. The butcher's dog, a Scottie, used to chase John if he heard the bells and then hang on to his trouser bottoms. Another dog also used to follow him, and John would run into the house panting, close the door quickly and stand behind it. "Oh Mum, it's that spotty dog, he won't leave me alone." Mum had to persuade John to leave his chaps off.

Peter, or Pip to us, bred rabbits when he was old enough, and he sold them for sixpence each. Pip was very enterprising, and after I was married and had Pauline, he baby-sat for me at 2/- per time while Mum and I went shopping. He would give us a time, but if I came back a bit late I had to pay him overtime. Pauline was always happy with him when he ran round with her in the pram.

In summer my brother John would go fishing or play football, and I would go with my school friends into the

19

hay fields where we played for hours, slinging one another into very large piles of hay. Then we would see how many different varieties of flowers we could find and name, and lie in the hay and listen to the skylarks — it all seemed like heaven. We played rounders and skipping on the spare ground, and sometimes our mothers would skip with us.

On other occasions we went to the top field where the miners used to let the pit ponies loose — this would happen on Friday nights, when they went wild, kicking their legs in the air, neighing and rolling in the grass. We were all fascinated and stood at the gate watching them. Then we would go to see the pigs and have a chat with them on an allotment near to our house. I loved pigs; they seemed to be so intelligent and would answer us back, or give us a sharp nip if they could.

The spare piece of ground came in very handy one week in the summer and one week in the autumn — it became a fairground, and it was right outside our back gate. There were small boat swings, roundabouts, dragons, a Noah's ark, and a beautiful carousel with horses. We knew the fairground people very well as they used to come every year. The villagers used to let them have water, and their caravans were beautiful — spotlessly clean and sparkling with cut glass and lovely large curtains. I used to wonder how they kept them so clean. I can still hear the fairground music in my mind — Albert bought me several records of it in later life. Mum used to make us come in for bed at ten o'clock, and I'd fall asleep listening to *Roses of Picardy* and

Souza's marches, and also the throb of the generators making the electricity. We always seemed to win a coconut, and we bought brandy snaps and toffee apples. We saved our coppers for these events, and we were sorry to see the fair leave.

Across the street from us was "Bobby Walker" the policeman's house. He was a large man, and when he told you not to do something that you were doing, you didn't do it. If it was foggy and he caught you out at night, he would tell you to get off home at once, and you did.

His daughter Audrey was my best friend — she was going to join up with me in the Air Force but she backed out, which didn't go down well with her Dad who was miffed. When I called for her one evening, he asked me in.

"When do you go, lass?" he asked. "Oh, next week, Mr Walker," I said.

He looked with scorn at Audrey. "I bet Jesse (my Dad) is very proud of his lass; she always did have brains." It was a nice compliment for me, but I did feel sorry for poor Audrey.

Audrey had two brothers and a sister. One brother, Billy, was roguish, and would go down to the bottom field with his friends and chase the horses about. He would grab their tails and run around with them, until one lashed out and he lost three front teeth. I wouldn't have liked to face his father, especially being the village policeman — in those days they had to be whiter than white, so Billy copped it.

During the war Billy was in the army and dropped over Arnhem, which was ambushed by the Germans. He was a POW and they were marched 200 miles. Many of them suffered terribly, but the irony was that Billy was killed in a car crash not long after the war. His brother Derek was different altogether. One was rough, the other brother was refined — Derek was a Petty Officer in the navy.

When my brother John was about 17 and Pip was 11, Dad bought two greyhounds, "Telegram" (or our name for him, "Bob"), and the younger "Blue Toledo" ("Bluey" to us). Bluey had yellow eyes and a bluey-grey coat, and he was beautiful and full of energy. Mum looked after their health and diet, as you had to be careful what you fed them when they were racing. She would clean their teeth, clip their nails, see to their ears etc. The boys trained them in the rec with a bicycle dragging a rabbit skin, and Dad gave advice. We raced Bob at Holmes, a small dog track which was near us. He did very well.

We managed to get Bluey a race at Owlerton, Sheffield. This was a large licensed track, and you were lucky if you managed to get your dog a race there. The time came for the race, and we were very excited. There were Pip and John, and I was there to back them up. The lads came back after seeing that the dog was all right. Two young men behind me were watching them parade the dogs around the ring.

"Whatever you do," one said to the other, "don't back that big grey dog, he's a fighter." People didn't back fighters.

I turned round and spoke to them. "Excuse me," I hissed at them, "you've got that one wrong. That grey dog is no fighter."

"How do you know?" they asked.

"He happens to be our dog, and you haven't seen him before because this is his first time out, right?" They looked at each other, then apologised.

When the race started, we were so excited. Bluey went like the wind and won by ten lengths — we couldn't get over it. As he was an outsider he was a big price, and we had put a bit of money on him, so we didn't do too badly. I turned round, and I shall never forget the look on the men's faces because they hadn't backed Bluey.

We arrived home elated. Mum was making our tea, and Dad was sat in his favourite chair smoking his little pipe full of fragrant tobacco (in which he used to put some whisky, and then heat it in a warm oven for a few minutes). Well, we waited with baited breath to tell him. "Pour the tea out, Ethel," he said, then turning to us, continued, "Now tell me all that happened." It all came out and we tried to tell him all at once what had happened. Dad beamed at us, "You've worked very hard," he said, "but you see, it worked out. I'm real proud of you all." We enjoyed our tea and gave the dog a big hug.

One day we were about to sit down for tea (we all sat down for our meals in those days), when the insurance man knocked on the door. It wasn't Mr Taylor, our usual insurance man, but a youngster, as Mr Taylor was ill. He came in, full of confidence, "Could I speak to

Jessie Overton to talk to her about her insurance please?"

"Am I the person you are seeking, young man?" Dad said in his best Micawber voice. "I am Jesse Nicholas Overton; note the spelling, J-E-S-S-E, I'm no Jessie." "Jessie" was the equivalent to "wally" to the cockneys, and in those days men were men.

"Sorry, Mr Overton, I'll remember next time," the young man said.

"Do that, young man, and we'll get on all right." Dad shook hands and the insurance man left feeling much better. Dad was proud of his name — in fact, we were all proud of his name, Jesse Nicholas Overton, it had such a nice ring to it. It didn't sound like a miner's name, as they were all Jack, Bill, Tom and Percy. My mum's name was Ethel May, but she hated it, so later on she dropped the Ethel as she preferred May. Dad called her Duck.

Every summer we would go to Kilnhurst, just outside Rotherham, to see the brass band contests. These were the miners' brass bands and they were excellent. It always seemed to be a fine day — everyone enjoyed themselves, and we would all arrive home very tired, going to sleep in no time at all.

One day Mum went to investigate why the gate kept opening and shutting, but nobody came in. She opened the gate quickly and the dog nearly fell in with the thing that he was pulling. Mum looked in horror because Digger had a large two-foot cod fish, complete with head and tail. He stood there, barked and wagged his tail. "Look what I've brought you," he was saying.

24

Mum was about to chastise him but thought better of it — she might confuse him. So she shouted for Dad.

"Oh my goodness, Duck, I know where he's got that from, the fish shop yard — I better go down and see Mr Bentley and pay for it" Mum was wondering how much it was going to cost, as it was such a large one. When Dad came back he was smiling — Mr Bentley had said that it was the fisherman's fault who had delivered it, as he had left the gates open. He said that Dad should clean it and skin it and it would be all right to eat. You couldn't waste anything in those days, and as we had no fridge we had to eat it for three days on the trot — fish and chips one day, fish cakes the next, and fish pie for the third.

We were used to this, as a joint of beef would be cooked for Sunday, cold meat and bubble and squeak would be served on Mondays, and hashed beef with cowheel in it was served with Yorkshire pudding on Tuesday. As we had plenty of vegetables from the garden we were all right.

The smells of my childhood stay with me, especially the nice ones — new mown hay, Mum's baking, oven-bottom cakes, fried onions, cucumber and spring onions, fish and chips with vinegar, roast beef or lamb on Sundays, and many more.

Anyway, getting back to Digger, he was becoming worse, chasing buses, bikes and cars up the lane, and going up to the farmer's field and chasing the cows and chickens. One day as the boys were coming through the gate he jumped it and nearly knocked them over. He dashed in the house, went behind the settee and stopped there all night. "What's he been up to?" Mum asked the lads. When they told her she said, "Oh, we can't have that, the hens will stop laying and the cows will stop giving milk." Dad got us all together and told us that we would have to part with Digger, so we all agreed, and a friend of Dad's at work took him. Digger went to obedience classes, but we were sorry to see him go because he was such a lovable rogue. Dad took him to his new home when we were all out so that we wouldn't get upset.

Sometimes I would go to Grandma Booker's in Denaby, eight miles away, for a week's holiday, and I used to look forward to this. Grandma was a little woman, about five foot two inches tall, and her name was Annie. She had three sons, all miners, and a daughter. These were my mother's half-brothers and half-sister — they were a lot younger than her, in fact they were not much older than my oldest brother. They were a lovely bunch of lads and they did all the housework between them when they came home from the pit. As it was a mining village they were a very close-knit community, and they had plenty of cousins around the same age, in their twenties. At night, if they didn't have any spending money left, they would play cards — on holiday they would play all night. I would sit on the settee and listen to them joking and laughing, and eventually I would fall asleep and one of them would cover me up with a shawl. Then another one would carry me upstairs and Gran would undress me and put me to bed.

They ordered their groceries from Brough's in town, and next day they would be delivered. I used to unpack the groceries and put them away — a dozen loaves (a baker's dozen which was 13), large tins of tomatoes, a big pack of bacon, a sack of potatoes; everything was big, as they were hard-working miners and had the appetites to match. Then we would go up to the farm to collect large new-laid eggs — it was all so exciting for me. Gran was always helping someone. She only had one lung, so that's why the children did all the work between them.

I made friends of my own age whilst I was there, and we played for hours in Conisborough Castle grounds. This was a lovely castle which fascinated me because it was so old. We used to tire ourselves out, and then we would go back to Gran's where I would sleep like a log through the night. When it was time to go home, Mum and Dad were always pleased to see me back, and Mum would smile and ask, "Enjoyed yourself, love?" I would reply, "I have, Mum, I have."

In 1937 I was 13 and I still read a lot about anything and everything — it was the Spanish Civil War this time. Dad would tell me what was going on, then he would buy a special war paper for 1d. I would read it, but it puzzled me, as I couldn't understand why they were fighting one another. "This is civil war," Dad said — little did I think that two years later we would have a war, but it wasn't fighting amongst ourselves. My imagination ran riot, as I tried to think what it was like to be bombed and to fight your own brothers and sisters, but I couldn't. Of course, all too soon, war clouds were looming in Britain.

I remember there was the crisis in 1938 — the Army came round with their large camouflaged lorries and collected the Territorial Army up first. They came for my oldest brother Ernest. He had his uniform on and his case packed in no time. It was thought that war was imminent. Chamberlain, the Prime Minister, believed he had peace in the bag, but he hadn't. Twelve months later war started, only this time it happened to be true.

The War Years

I had started work in 1938, leaving school at the age of 14. I had about six jobs in 18 months, each job worse than the last, and I received very little money — not enough to keep children in crisps and pop nowadays.

The first job I had was in a fishing tackle shop, working in the back of the premises sorting out maggots. The van would deliver the maggots into a big empty bath and I would sort them out into smaller baths — big ones in the right, small ones in the left, and dead husks in the bin. Then I had to put them in clean bran so that they were then ready — all of this for eight shillings per week . . . and I worked 52 hours!

My next job was cleaning in a bakery and grocery shop. Sometimes I had to dunk legs of ham and bacon, that hung from the ceiling in mutton cloth, into buckets of boiling water for a few seconds to drown the maggots on them — "Oh brother, wasn't I ever going to get away from maggots!" "Joan, give your notice in and look for another job," were my mother's favourite words.

I always remember the 3rd September 1939 — the exact time and place. Mum was baking, Dad was mending shoes, and I was putting Blanco on some plimsolls. As I was sat on the step I remember listening to the wireless playing music. The time was nearly eleven o'clock. All of a sudden Big Ben struck the hour, and a solemn voice came over the air, saying that we were at war with Germany. It went terribly quiet for a few minutes, and then we all came to and spoke at once. War, war, war — what did it mean?

I sat and thought about it. I could hear Mum and Dad discussing it, and my mind was going into overdrive. I was imagining it like a film I had seen, something like *War of the Worlds*. I had seen pictures of the Air Force and decided that was what I wanted to be in — they were all such gentlemen. I had to patiently wait until I was 17 — and then I applied. In the meantime, the Army had come with their lorries to collect Ernest again. This time he was in the Army proper and was issued with pith helmet, puttees, etc, so he was being sent overseas. We didn't hear a word from him for three weeks, and Mum and Dad were very worried, thinking that he was on the high seas. Then one teatime while we were eating, in Ernest walked. We all had tears in our eyes.

"Oh, where have you been, son?" asked Dad. "At Greasborough, Dad," my brother answered, "On the 'Ack-Ack' guns."

This was only about three miles away. When we realized what had happened, we saw the funny side of it and laughed and laughed. The war was on, mail had been stopped in case any word got to the enemy, and we were very spy-conscious in those days.

The firm that Ernest had worked for as an engineer before he went into the Forces was Vickers Armstrong, one of the main works at the time, so they applied for my brother's release and got it as he had an important job.

My father went to join up, but he was also exempt as he was a miner, so he had to stay down the pit. Later Dad had some kind of accident and managed to get out of the pit into the steelworks, but he had been down the pit for 29 years, which was a long time. He would find a big difference between the pit and the steelworks.

Just before I joined up in the Air Force, we had been given an Anderson shelter. Dad had put it in the middle of the garden, and it didn't look very nice stuck there like a brown carbuncle, covered in soil, so I decided to decorate it. I set Virginia stock seeds in the middle, spelling my name all across it, with mauve-scented stock around the outside to frame it. The first leave I had I came home to such a beautiful sight, my name standing out like a beacon of flowers! The disappointment was that Dad explained that we had to dig it all up as we might be accused of being spies, living near the big steel works, with my name looking like a signal to the Germans. So I gave it one long last look and then destroyed it, and then planted green shrubs instead.

We didn't go short of much during the war as we swapped eggs for a quarter pound of tea etc now and then. I used to have to count these eggs every day and record them on a ruled piece of paper on the back of a cupboard door. This was to see which birds weren't up to scratch. Then Mum would give them a dose of Karswood Spice, and that would do the trick.

At Christmas we sold the poultry, and I watched Dad with amusement one time when he took the hatchet with him across the spare ground to our allotment and put the tree stump ready (we could see him from our house). Then he proceeded to chase the hens round the garden. After about half an hour he caught one. He raised the hatchet, but when we opened our eyes he hadn't done anything. He then called me over and said, "Pidge, fetch the farmer's boy — everybody to their own job," and with that he disappeared down the pub for a pint . . . it must have been thirsty work chasing hens around! We never let him see us laugh, or that would have lowered his dignity. We then plucked and dressed the chickens.

When the war had been going for about twelve months, I was 16 and working in a silversmiths and cutlers warehouse. When I arrived home from work one night I told Mum that I was going with some girls from work to the Sheffield Empire to see Henry Hall and his band. We had been saving our coppers up at work for weeks, and it was close to Christmas. She said, "You are not going anywhere tonight, my girl. Lord Haw-Haw says the Germans are going to bomb us tonight. I was going to a dance tonight, too, but I'm not going and you're not going either."

I replied, "You don't take any notice of him do you? He's rubbish." Mum gave me one of her freezing looks, and I shut up. It came to the allotted time, and nothing happened. I looked up and said, scornfully, "I told you he was rubbish, didn't I?" Then all of a sudden there was a drone, an almighty bang, and the Blitz had started. I also received an almighty crack from Mum for being cheeky. We were about four miles away so we only heard the bombing and saw the red sky.

My mother was making tea and sandwiches as usual when the air-raid started. "Joan, tomorrow you hand in your notice and look for another job."

Famous last words. Next day she waltzed me up to Sheffield, where we managed to get to the Wicker Arches but we couldn't get any further. The devastation was horrifying, with unexploded bombs everywhere and piles and piles of rubble so that it was hard to see the streets — or Sheffield. We were talking to a policeman who advised us to go home, and he told us that Marples, the hotel where Mum had been going to the dance, had experienced a direct hit — hundreds sheltering in the basement were killed. When she went back to work some of Mum's friends were missing. I apologised.

I had no job so I stayed at home to look after my two younger brothers while Mum kept on working at the steelworks, Steel, Peech and Tozer. It was while Mum was there that she met Arnold Jackson. He worked with Mum on cranes at the steel works, before he joined the Air Force. He used to see me sometimes waiting for her coming out of work.

One day this airman came down our path, and I said, "Do we know any airmen, Mum?"

"Not that I know of," she replied, but when she looked at him properly, she said, "Why, it's Spike."

(Spike was his nickname at work.) Mum introduced us, and his eyes lit up when he saw me. Arnold was 18 and I was 16. Mum gave him a cup of tea and we sat chatting.

Arnold told us that he was on sick leave. Some of the airmen had been sleeping in tents, but when there was a thunderstorm the tent became flooded. They slept like logs all the way through it; Arnold ended up with rheumatic fever, so they discharged him, unfit for service. He wasn't given any compensation, just so many weeks of sick leave. We liked each other and started courting. Eventually Arnold joined the Army, although he didn't say anything to me, he just signed up.

One night Mum was on "nights" and Dad was on "days". It was about 5.30 in the morning when there was a loud knock at the door. A few minutes went by, then Dad came upstairs. "Pidge love, your Mum's had an accident, she's fell out of the crane and fell into a tool box. There was an air raid."

My heart stopped. "Is she dead, Dad?"

"No, love, she's all right, she isn't hurt." I couldn't believe it, I'd seen those cranes, about 30 to 40 feet high. He assured me she was all right, that she'd only dislocated her shoulder and they had put it right. She must have been made of rubber.

As soon as I reached the age of 17 — I joined the Air Force. Arnold didn't like it at all, and told me off. I should have known what he was like, but they say that love is blind — well, it sure was. Being shy, gentle and naïve, I didn't realise what was happening.

Mum took me to the recruitment centre in Cambridge Street, Sheffield, and within a fortnight I was in the Royal Air Force. They didn't mess about in those days you know! I was sent a railway pass and a certain amount of money — not a lot — and told which train to catch to Gloucester.

I went to the station on my own as I didn't like saying goodbye, crying, and all that stuff. I'd never been on a train before, so it was all new. I gave the man on the gate my ticket and he told me what platform I wanted. He could see that I was apprehensive, so he said, "Follow those girls in front, they're going to the same place." I thanked him and went on my way. I kept my eye on them all the time and wouldn't go to sleep in case I passed my station.

When we arrived a sergeant herded us together and we went in RAF buses to the camp. The camp was enormous. I hadn't seen anything like it in my life — girls marching on the square, and a sergeant shouting weird things at them. I was thinking to myself what would happen if you didn't stop when he shouted, "Halt," or what would happen if he shouted, "Right turn," and you turned left. I had that to find out.

The next day we had our inoculations etc, and we were marched to another hut for X-rays. Oh boy, was I embarrassed. We were all lined-up, and the woman sergeant shouted, "All clothes off, but your pants on." As I was very modest I put my shirt round my shoulders. There was a bellow down my right ear, "You, Airwoman, shirt off, head up, shoulders back, stomach in." So I stood there with my hands across my chest. I

35

turned round a bit and looked up the room. I'd never seen so many boobs in my life, talk about big ones, small ones, some as big as your head, as the old song goes, and I felt a lot better as I was average. I always had a sense of humour, so what made me smile to myself was all the pants we wore — directoire knickers ("passion killers") they were called, made out of silk in Air Force blue with elasticated legs, the ones old ladies wore. Oh boy, did we look a right bunch of 'nanas.

I soon had the smile wiped off my face. The female doctor went for her dinner and a tall, handsome male doctor took over. How I blushed when he said, "Come along, Airwoman, it won't take long," and then he smiled which made me blush all the more. "That didn't hurt, did it?" he said, but I was glad to escape.

The next day we sorted out uniforms and careers. We were all marched to the stores where we were given uniforms, shoes, a tin mug, knife, fork and spoon. When we finished a meal we had to wash them outside in a trough full of hot water. We all looked at one another in disgust. I used to wash mine again when we got back to our huts. The uniforms were either too big or too small. I managed to swap mine with a bigger girl, so I was lucky. We were all used to wearing high-heeled shoes and we were issued with flat leather lace-ups, and how we had blisters after marching up and down!

The careers officer asked us what we wanted to do. I said drive or hair-dressing. It didn't matter what we wanted to do — we all ended up on barrage balloons. These were used to prevent the Luftwaffe from flying too low. The balloons were flown to about 1,000 feet and two small explosive devices were attached to the bottom and top of the wire. Any aircraft flying too low would hit the wires, causing the small explosives to detonate, so bringing down the plane. These were very effective, as I saw on many occasions.

While you are in the Air Force, you learn a lot.

The first lesson we learned was never to complain. My three friends and I were having dinner one day when the Duty Officer and Sergeant came round.

"Any complaints, Airwomen?" he smiled at us.

"Yes, sir," said Lilian, "we don't like the potatoes looking at us while we are eating." (She meant the eyes on the potatoes.) "Right, girls," he said, still smiling, "report to the cook house at nine o'clock in the morning — you, you, you and you." The four of us reported to the smiling Sergeant the next morning, who ordered us to follow him. I was thinking, "Why do Sergeants and Corporals smile at Airwomen?" I soon found out.

"There you are, girls," he said, handing us a small kitchen knife each. He knocked on the wall, and down a chute came a ton of spuds that needed eyeing. "And don't forget, take every eye out, and report to me when you have finished."

When we finished those, we rubbed our hands, pleased with what we had done, when bump, another load came down the chute, and we were there all day, going for meals in pairs. I couldn't face potatoes for a while after that!

After our six week training and passing-out parade, we were posted to Norton Aerodrome, Sheffield, where we were sent on a course. We were in large hangars, a certain number on each balloon. We had to learn how to patch them, repair them, fill them with gas, let them up and down, and how to handle the large concrete blocks that anchored the balloon. Essie Spaver from Doncaster, one of our bright sparks, forgot to let go of the rope when she was told to. She sailed to the top of the hangar so that only the bottom of her shoes were showing. When we hauled her down we started laughing and couldn't stop, until we were threatened with being put on a charge by the instructor — then we shut up!

Going back to the camp after a 24-hour leave one night, I proceeded along the bottom of Dixon Lane. The blackout was on, and as I passed the public house on the corner the door opened, the blackout curtains parted, and this big man staggered out the worse for drink. "Ha, ha, I'm having you," he said as he leered towards me with his arms outstretched — I went cold. "No, you're not," I shouted, and I hit him with a jar of marmalade Mum had given me. We called it marmalade but it was made of all sorts in those days. Anyway, he yelled and ran up the street. Another man came running towards me and I said, "You as well?" He went pale and said, "No, no, I've come to help." He seemed genuine so I thanked him and went on my way. When I got to where my bus was waiting, I looked down at my coat, and it was covered in bits of peel and whatnots. My hair and hat were the same.

I had to walk half a mile in the blackout to the guardhouse when I got off the bus, so I was still wary of anything untoward. When I came to the guardhouse I nearly fell in with relief. The two corporals looked at me with surprise, and one of them asked, "Ee, what's happened to you, lass?" So I explained everything. "Bully for you, at least you can look after yourself," he replied. "If it was only with marmalade, you must have given him what for, serves him right" When I looked I'd still got the jar in my hand — well, half a jar, the top had come off, so I must have given him such a belt with it! They cleaned me up with a damp cloth and gave me the usual mug of tea with plenty of sugar in it, and we had a good laugh about the incident. I trotted off feeling a lot better. My friends had a good laugh when I got back to the billet, but I was very cautious when I passed that place again.

From there we were sent to Brocco Bank on a balloon opposite the botanical gardens. One night a large lorry was parked overnight in a small lane beside us — the driver had permission to leave it there. Being inquisitive, next morning I asked him what load he was carrying. "Explosives," was the reply. We all looked at him, shocked, and this brought home to us the realities of war.

From Sheffield we were posted to Glasgow. It was winter and we arrived in Glasgow at night. Next morning when we were paraded outside for our duties we got the shock of our lives to find that we were in the middle of the Gorbals, a most infamous place. It was a square of black tenements with half the windows out; children, ragged with no shoes on, running round stealing everything that wasn't fastened down. We had

39

to watch the balloon 24 hours a day. I cried that night, praying that we weren't going to stay there. The first thing I learnt was to stand with my back against a wall while I was on guard, so that nobody would creep up behind me. The shift we did was two hours on and four hours off. That two hours on seemed like a week.

We had only been there a few days when a drunk going back to his ship on the Clyde, which wasn't very far away, hit one of our girls on the back of her head with a bottle, and she had to be taken to hospital. The next day we were transferred to Pollockshields, the residential part of Glasgow, in Maxwell Park. That was very nice, and what a relief.

One day when things were quiet there was a sharp noise. Someone had fired an air rifle at the balloon, thinking that it would explode, but they must have been disappointed because the pellet went through one side and came out the other. The only problem was that we had to ground it, empty the helium out, and patch the holes. What a job. So we now had to be aware of anyone snooping about with an air rifle.

At the end of March, Arnold sent me a telegram:

"Get home to get married. Embarkation leave."

I went to head office to ask the officer in charge for permission. He refused, saying he had a daughter my age, and he didn't think that I was old enough. So that was that. When you're in the Forces, you have to accept all that's thrown at you, with no answering back. So I sent a telegram back, saying "Refused permission". But next morning a messenger came — the CO had changed his mind and sent me permission, a railway pass and ration money, 30 shillings. So I sent another telegram:

"Will arrive home tonight. Love Joan"

When I arrived home I had to ask my Dad's permission. He said no, not until I was 21. Oh boy, what now? Anyway, Arnold, his Mum and my Mum all had a chat with Dad, and he reluctantly said yes. We asked the canon's permission to get a special licence, and we were married two days later.

Now comes the crunch. On the great day, the parson didn't turn up, so two of the congregation went to fetch him from home, which wasn't far away, and he came all in a flurry. He hadn't been advised of our wedding by the canon. My bridesmaid, Dora, Arnold's cousin, turned up dressed all in black, including a black veil, as her husband had just been killed in the desert. I'm sure my marriage was doomed from the start.

After our leave we went to the station and we sat in the waiting room holding hands and kissing. It reminds me of that film, *Brief Encounter*. Arnold boarded the train first, to Gravesend, as he was headed to Burma, so we kissed and waved goodbye. But about a dozen soldiers waved me goodbye, so I could only just see Arnold as the train went through the tunnel. Then I caught my train to Glasgow, feeling down in the dumps.

When I arrived back at the balloon site everything was quiet, with only the Airwoman on duty at the gate. I went into the dining room where we used to sit and play records, talk, write letters and read. There wasn't a sound. It seemed ever so weird. Then all of a sudden the lights came on (paraffin lamps), there were about 30 people and the music started. I shall always remember Joe Loss's band playing *In the Mood*. It was an old gramophone with a brass horn, as we had no electricity. As they sang "For she's a jolly good fellow", I had a lump in my throat as this was the first party I'd ever had. They even came from head office and other sites.

This party was for my wedding and my 18th birthday, which had been a few weeks before. I was the youngest on site. We had trestle tables put end-to-end down the room, groaning with food and presents that they had brought. I was given *Evening in Paris* perfume, Coty face powder with a fancy puff, and all sorts. I marvelled at them because such things were so hard to get during wartime. Even two off-duty policemen came with a large cream cake — that was a miracle as there was no cream to be had — and a very large lump of coal, as we were getting short of that too. You didn't ask questions in those days, you just accepted gracefully. The police used to walk round our railings during the night and we used to give them a mug of tea or Oxo with a thick slice of toast. They were good friends.

Some days when I was on an early, it would be breaking daylight and there would be a mist (Scotch mist they called it). The balloon would be resting on top of the mist, gently swaying, and looking like a giant silver egg — I would look awestruck at the beautiful sight. At other times we would have a gale and rain, and we had to go into the night in raincoats and sou'westers to anchor the balloon so it wouldn't blow away. The concrete blocks were very heavy (112 lb) but they would sway in the wind, so we had to be very careful they didn't catch us — they could lay you out. When we eventually finished we were exhausted and would go inside, peel off our wet clothes, and sit round the pot-bellied stove hugging a pint pot of steaming tea and a thick slice of toast.

We took it in turns to be cook; everybody did a week at a time. Oh boy, some of them were terrible cooks, they'd burn everything. I wasn't a bad cook, so the corporal let us swap. I always changed with a girl called Campion who could even burn water. The girls loved my meat and potato pie, rice pudding, and jam roly-poly.

We had to make-do with rations from headquarters; we always had plenty of potatoes, carrots, dried peas and dried eggs — the things you could make with these ingredients! The only thing was that you had to have a good imagination. You also had to get up at 5.30 a.m. to get the stove working — it was a large iron one with two ovens and four rings on top. If you didn't clean the thing out properly, clinkers and all, it smoked all day and everything tasted of smoke — even the water for the tea. This was survival. That is why even today I can turn my hand to all sorts. "Never stick fast" was my motto.

One night I was on guard at about midnight; one of the girls had mashed a pot of tea for me before they went to bed — they'd left cups, milk and sugar. I nipped in to get a cup, and I thought that I would empty the large teapot to help those doing breakfasts. It was blackout and I had a torch turned on which I held under my arm. So I called out for anyone going to the toilets, which were outside, "Look out, tea coming over!" This is what we all used to do as we would sling the spent tea-leaves into the hedge, as there were no grates or running water.

I was stood on the steps of the cook house, and in walked the duty officer. I was paralysed. I was in for it now, as I had caught him with the tea leaves in the chest down his great coat. I rushed inside to get a clothes brush and a clean tea cloth to dust him down with. It's a good job there wasn't much liquid in the pot. I was waiting for the bellow of "Airwoman". But when I looked up I found that he was laughing. I'm glad it wasn't a female officer who was on night duty, she probably would have had me court-martialled for assaulting an officer and insulting the King's uniform, and sent to the Tower for hanging. The women officers were more severe than the men, that's why we didn't like them coming round; some could really be very arrogant.

This officer said, "Ah, tea, have you a cup to spare?"

"Certainly, sir," I answered. No damage was done, and he was still smiling when we drank our tea, keeping our eyes on the balloon out of the window in the moonlit sky as best we could. He said to me, "Well, Airwoman, I thought I was going to have a boring night, but I haven't." He remembered me from the 18th birthday party. As he went through the door, he said, "Well, goodnight, Airwoman." We saluted each other. The only thing that I had forgotten was that I was in the small passage and so I banged all my fingers on the wall. "I think I'd better go before you knock the joint down, Airwoman," and I could see by his torch light he was still smiling to himself. I never forgot that night.

Anyway, about three months on, two important-looking officers with clipboards took us into the dining room one at a time and gave us an intelligence test. We were curious to know what it was all about, but we found out two days later.

Four of us had passed, and they wanted us to train as flight mechanics on aero engines. What did I know about aero engines? I had never seen one. I had only seen a plane in the sky. Well, ours was not to reason why, so we packed our kit bags and headed for St Athans, Cardiff.

This was a very large aerodrome, the largest in the world at one time. There was a cinema, roller skating rink, dance hall, baths, showers, wooden huts, the lot — we thought we were in Shangri-La. After a short session of marching back and forth we settled down to some hard grafting. The course was condensed into six months, although it should have been longer. As it was wartime they were short of mechanics, so that was it.

When the Air Force said that you were going to learn something, you did, and you didn't pass until you were up to standard. We had to learn everything about engines — how to take them to pieces, and of course put them back together, metallurgy, splicing ropes and wire, tying knots, running engines up, and guiding the planes in and out of their bases. The hardest part was running the engines up. Some of us couldn't do it — the noise was horrendous, and through this we had to check all the instruments. This took some doing as the noise took your mind off things. We had to learn to swing a propeller into action — which was really frightening, because if you slipped and fell into it you were chopped into pieces, and so we were very careful! About half of the course didn't pass as they were too frightened.

We had to do practical and theory, but I couldn't swot too much because I'd lose my concentration. So I would read part of a book two or three times and then go to the pictures. I found that it would then sink in. They said that I wouldn't pass, but I did. One of my friends Lilian had a brainstorm when we had finished due to too much swotting.

All four of us passed and then we had 14 days leave. The medical officer said that Lilian would be all right after a few days away from the course, so we carted her between us down to the railway station. She was like a zombie, and we laid her on a luggage rack with a greatcoat under her head and covered her with other coats. She slept all the way to Leeds, where we arrived at her sister's house, who made us very welcome. We stayed the night and then went home.

After our leave, we were sent to Newcastle to work on Spitfires. I loved them — they were Rolls Royce engines and we soon got used to them. It was summer, so we all serviced our "kites" (that's what we called the planes) and then we would all sit outside on the grass and sunbathe, waiting for them to come back. It was a lovely summer.

During my time in the Air Force, Mr Milsom the butcher used to make me a large 7 lb pork pie every time I came home on leave, and I even had a Gunstones cream cake from his grocer's shop. The pork pie fitted in a very large round biscuit tin, and to go with it was a large jar of pickled onions that Mum had made. Together these weighed a ton, but I always managed to stagger back to camp with them. When I took them down to the squadron, my friends would all be waiting there with open arms. We used to count everybody, even the sergeant, and we would cut the slices accordingly. Then came the pickled onions, of which we all were very fond. The strong smell of onions filled the air, but everyone was satisfied. Everyone shared their parcels like this — we were all one big happy family.

As winter approached, so came the rain and gales as we were near the North Sea. When this happened we had to be ballast for the Spitfires. This meant that as the kites were going down for take-off, we had to sit on the tail with one arm around the fuselage. Just before the pilot gathered speed we banged on the fuselage and he would slow down so that we could jump off. Well, at least that was the theory, and it worked well in most instances. However, on one occasion the pilot didn't slow down as he had a hangover from the night before. I knew that I had to get off quickly or I would have gone up, so I had to think fast, and get under the slip-stream which came from the propeller and kept you on the plane. I had to be quick, and no messing. So with one burst of adrenaline I pushed myself off and rolled onto the grass verge and stayed there.

They had been watching this from the tower, and all came dashing across to help. They picked me up, but my legs were like jelly. I looked at my new mittens but all the front of them was gone, and my coat sleeves were also damaged. Anyway, I soon recovered after they plied me with the remedy for everything — a cup of hot tea with plenty of sugar. The pilot was put on a charge. They asked me if I wanted him to be court-martialled and I said no, I was just glad to be alive. However, he was charged with being careless and endangering a life. He was fined, the money was given to me, and I put it in the kitty. There was a barn not far from us where they held barn-dances, so that's where we went to enjoy ourselves on the money in the kitty.

It was around this time that I was promoted to LACW, Leading Aircraft Woman. I was delighted and it entitled me to a propeller badge on my sleeve. Dad was ecstatic when I went home, but it's a shame that Arnold didn't feel the same way. All I got from him was, "You would, wouldn't you?" It was like throwing a bucket of cold water over me. You see, he was still a private, so he

48

was jealous of me getting promotion. I didn't tell him I was Acting Corporal, and I didn't go in for the corporal tests as I couldn't upset him any more.

No wonder later in life I had enough and the worm turned. Dad never did like Arnold, and on my wedding day he had tears in his eyes as he gave me away. When we went into the vestry, he whispered to me, "You will get hurt, Pidge, but we will be there to pick up the pieces." He was so right.

One day I had two kites to see to, so I gave them their daily inspection and was just rubbing my hands together, pleased with myself, when the sergeant came out.

"Jacko, do me a favour will you? Will you service this kite for me? It's come out of the hangar after a major inspection. Shouldn't take long." (I was always called "Jacko", being Jackson; anyone called White was always "Chalkie".) I was miffed. "Sarge, I've just done two."

"Well, you are the only one I can depend on, I can't depend on them," he said pointing to two cockney lads. Well, neither could I; one of them had left a spanner in a kite — it's a good job it came down all right. I wouldn't trust them with anything of mine as they were always larking about. Anyway, I did it and I took my time. The sergeant came out and asked me if I'd finished, so I said, "Won't be long, Sarge," and tested everything I could lay my hands on. This kite had had a major inspection and every part had been renewed. I signed for it, which meant that if anything happened I was responsible, and could be court-martialled if anything went wrong.

We stood watching it take off, but as it got up speed and took off, it suddenly nose-dived into snow in the next field. We were flabbergasted and dashed across the field to the Polish pilot who we thought was dead. Thankfully he wasn't, and he sat there with a lump on his forehead where he had banged it against a gadget encased in rubber. He was dazed, but otherwise all right. It was the pilot I had been worrying about, not the kite.

I had to go in front of four officers sat behind a large desk. They asked me what I had done on my inspection. So I told them, and this was backed up by the sergeant. Anyway, we all had to go out onto the field to find the split-pin from the throttle which had been the cause of the trouble. I thought it was hopeless, like looking for a needle in a haystack.

The Steam Jennies got to work melting the snow, and we all had to start looking. We were lucky and soon found one half near the plane, but the second half was a bit elusive. Anyway, we were all getting tired when someone shouted, "It's here!" Was I glad. When I looked at it I couldn't believe that such a little thing could cause so much trouble. It looked new at both ends but was rusty in the middle, which was why I couldn't see the problem — they should have changed it in the hangar.

When I think back, we were very lucky that the plane hadn't caught fire. The pilot was all right after a short stay in hospital and they had stopped flying for the day because of the snow. That left us free to search, and the investigation cleared me of negligence. Did I sleep well that night! However, I did get my leg pulled by the lads. "Jacko, I can see you doing jankers for life." Another one said, "Jacko, you'll have to pay for that a tanner a week until you're old and grey." Oh boy, I'd still be paying!

While we were on Spitfires in Newcastle, another incident happened. An American plane requested to land, but he had a bomb fastened underneath. We were only a fighter base, and he was a bomber, so he would only just be able to land. Anyway, he changed his mind as one side of the bomb attachment had come loose, so he was ordered to go over the sea and try to shake it off. It was the North Sea, and not very far away. We managed to get the rest of our aircraft airborne, and he came back, thankfully after having dumped the bomb. This time he managed to land, but not before we had rushed down into the shelter, as we weren't taking any chances — he was too big for our runway. Anyway, he managed it, and we all breathed a sigh of relief.

Another time an American fighter landed. The aircrew got out of their plane and walked past my Spitfire. One of the airmen looked up and saw me sat astride my kite, putting petrol in. "Oh! A dame!" He was surprised. "I can't believe it, wait until I write and tell Mom." So he whipped a camera out of his jacket and took my photo.

"Don't do that," I said, "you'll get into trouble, you're breaking the secrets code." I don't think he believed me.

"See you tonight in the canteen, sister, and I'll bring you some barley sugars." I wondered what he thought he was going to get for barley sugars! He waved and shouted, "See you at seven," and I thought to myself, "No, you won't." I didn't trust Americans. I thought of the saying, "Overpaid, over-sexed and over here". I might have got things wrong, but I still didn't trust them.

Another time, I went to fasten a French pilot in — just as I walked towards the plane, the pilot had his back to me and was urinating on the tail unit — I nearly burst a gasket. The blooming cheek! I had cleaned it beforehand with petrol, and it shone. I was proud of my two kites and kept them nice and clean, so I tore him off a strip. He threw his hands in the air and apologised profusely, so I accepted his apology and fastened him in. Gosh, he didn't know how much he had ruffled my feathers. When he came back he smiled at me and said in broken English, "You forgive?" and I smiled back and said, "Yes." My planes were called "F" for Freddy, and "P" for Pete.

We never did like church parades — one or two of us hid in the wardrobes. I could hear the sergeant clomping around the huts. He stopped outside my wardrobe, my heart thumped, and I thought I was going to have a heart attack anyway, someone called him away, and I breathed a sigh of relief. "Never again, never again," I said to myself, and it taught me a lesson.

When you started work each morning, you didn't know what was round the corner, and there was always an incident of some kind. My friend and oppo, Bob Bruce (I always called him Robert the Bruce as he

52

came from north of the border) and I were laughing about something as we were walking up to the cookhouse. We looked up to see a Spitfire that was in the circuit to land, when an American Mustang cut straight across the circuit, against all regulations, and they collided. We stood aghast. They disintegrated, and the wings came down in slow motion, like the seeds floating down from a Sycamore tree. We made our way up to the crash, when all of a sudden there were loud explosions, sounding like ammunition going off. We dived into a gutter, and when we thought it was all clear, we proceeded up the hill for our dinner — we couldn't do anything. It had been like a nightmare, and it didn't finish there, as the next day we had to go in what we called the "blood wagon" to see if we could find any parts of bodies, which had been scattered over a large area. We only found bits of the planes. I was praying I didn't find heads or anything like that. Someone did, about a fortnight afterwards, in a stream about a mile away. One tragic mistake, which only took a few seconds, and two young men lost their lives — that's war, anything could happen, and it did. I thought of the saying, "Live for today, for tomorrow you may die". I put it out of my mind and got on with the job in hand.

As I was Acting Corporal, sometimes I had to be on guard duty in the guardroom at night. Once when I went to report back on the airfield I was a few minutes late, and I was bawled-out by a large red-haired female sergeant. "You're late, Airwoman."

"Sorry, Sergeant," I replied, "I've been on night duty in the guardroom."

"We will have no excuses, you're late. Don't let it happen again."

I had missed my breakfast and hadn't had much sleep, so I was in a wicked mood. I set my face and thought to myself, "She can't stop me from thinking that she is a big, fat red-headed bladder of lard, she must be crackers."

"Did you say something, Airwoman?" she bellowed down my ear.

"No, Sergeant," I answered. She said something else, but I didn't hear her, I'd shut off. After that any sergeant shouting things at us was automatically shut off — that's what meditation does for you, and I can still do it today.

After so long on Spitfires, we were posted to Gosport just outside Portsmouth. When we arrived we were shocked to find that Portsmouth had been bombed to the ground and most of the shops were single-storey buildings made out of corrugated iron. We arrived there and after a meal were directed to our new squadron. After booking in at the guardroom, the sergeant said to us, "I think you've got the wrong place, we don't have WAAFs on this squadron, they are all men."

"Well, I'm afraid you're stuck with us, Sarj," I said. We had got there before the report about us had arrived.

"Well, I don't know what I'm going to do with you, I'm sure," he said. As I was a Leading Aircraft Woman, I had our papers, and looking shocked the sergeant said, "Women flight mechanics; I didn't know there were any. Let's see what you can do." With a grin on his face, he shouted to one of the lads. "Jones, this is your new oppo, Jacko."

I nearly fainted when I saw the planes were Lancasters. As I was only five foot four and only about eight stone, the wheels were nearly as big as me. We didn't see the planes until we had gone through the building to the other side. Anyway, we had two engines each, so I climbed the steps and started the inspection. It was a good job that heights didn't bother me. The thought of being up there (they are almost as big as a house) could make me faint now.

When I had finished, I sat in the cockpit and sized up the panel — there seemed to be hundreds of gauges. Dad had taught me to simplify things, so in my mind I thought I only had two engines, not four, and then classed them as two Spitfire engines. So I looked through the window and shouted "All clear," and "All clear" came back. I ran it up all right. As we had no ear-muffs in those days, we had to contend with the noise, and I had learnt how to think through it. I have bad tinnitus now, so this helps me a lot. I helped my oppo do his engines by taking the covers off, putting them on the ground and seeing that everything was all clear. When we had finished we went in to sign and the sergeant asked how I'd done. "OK," said my oppo, "I think she knows more than me. By the way, what kites have you been on, Jacko?" I replied, "Spitfires." They were astonished. "Spitfires" was a magical word, everybody loved them, and so we were accepted and they were friendly and helped us a lot.

As the time for demob came, everyone was excited. I had my rose-coloured specs on, thinking about being reunited with my tall, dark and handsome husband, getting a comfortable little house with a lovely little garden, having a couple of kids and my husband having a secure job. We had been parted three-and-a-half years, which was a long time when you are young and in love.

Married Life

I was demobbed about three months before my husband, so I went and got my old job back temporarily until he came home. The job was at Pinders, the silversmiths and cutlers warehouse that before the Sheffield Blitz was at the bottom of the moor. It was so different from the RAF, but at least I was still saving up for a house. I had saved all the time I had been in the Air Force, putting away my husband's allowance, and the money from tailoring alterations I did from time to time — I used to alter trousers, skirts etc, while my friends and I sat round the fire talking instead of going out.

They had built some new houses in the village where I lived — two-bedroom houses for £200, three-bedroom for £300, and I meant to have one. It was hard to get a mortgage in those days. We also had our name on the Rotherham housing list. We had had our names down for four years and the points added up, so we were near the top. However, we were not offered anything, and when I enquired I discovered that we were moving further down the list as people with children were being given priority.

I had reached the allotted goal of £200, but I needed about £50 for solicitor's fees etc. It doesn't seem a lot nowadays but it was a small fortune and it would take quite a time to save up for it — after all, I was only earning £2.18s a week. We were going to live with my in-laws in a shop they were buying in Rotherham until we got a house. The shop was a general store, selling food, sweets, cigarettes etc, which were all still rationed.

So back to work I went until my husband came home. I went to the station to fetch him, and when he alighted from the train I stopped in my tracks and stared at him. I hardly recognised him — he was over six foot, he'd broadened out, grown a moustache and he was in khaki uniform and a large bush hat. I became shy at first, it was like looking at a stranger. Anyway, after sitting on a bench kissing and talking, we seemed to be all right and we went to my parents' home where my furniture was until the shop was in order. So I went back to work for a few weeks, and that's when I met the "Buffers".

One day when I was wiping tablespoons, I had to take about a dozen back to the buffers to redo as there was a mark on them. So I innocently went up the stairs to the top floor; though I'd worked there before, I'd never been upstairs. I opened the door and walked in. Well, I thought I'd died and gone to hell. Everything was black, and only little glimmers of light came through the windows as they were filthy — there was dirt all over the place and the noise was tremendous. The women were singing and seemed happy enough, and they all wore red headscarves covering all their hair, brown paper aprons round their legs, and rags round their fingers. I'd never seen anything like it.

I ventured up to the first woman and explained in a timid voice that the spoons just wanted touching up. "Who the f***ing heck sent these?"

"Me," I said.

"Well, don't bring any f***ing more," she shouted, along with a few more select phrases. I thought she'd gone mad. It touched a raw nerve. As I didn't swear, I shouted back, "I'll bring you a flaming gross back next time and you'll have something to whinge about." She stopped dead and then put her arm up. I thought she was going to strike me, thinking, "You do and you'll be flat on your back before you know where you are, mate." Anyway, she didn't, she put her arm around my shoulder and shouted to the others, "One of us, lasses. Doris, bring her a mug of tea. Do you take sugar, lass?"

She asked me where I had worked before because I was a new face. I told her the Air Force, and she asked what I did there. I explained about being a mechanic on aero-engines, and she was amazed, forgetting to swear for a bit. She passed all this on to her mates who were also amazed. I must explain, they were well known for swearing, and they were straight "John Bull" and tough. No wonder people were frightened of them, but they could be very kind and generous, and helped one another. So after that I was always welcomed and I used to take up some of the other girls' "cuckoos" (rejects) because they didn't like being there. However, I still thought I wouldn't like to be a buffer for anything, even if I was destitute, but I had to have second thoughts about this later on due to my circumstances.

Eventually I left there and went to live in my in-laws' shop, and my husband went back to the job he had before his army days. He was a fireman with the railway, earning £5 per week, less stamps. After paying for our lodgings, bus fares etc, we were left with a few shillings. My mother-in-law and I came to an agreement that I would work in the shop to augment our rent. We opened until 8.30 at night because we were near the theatre and picture houses, and we sold chocolate, sweets and cigarettes, all on coupons, which was tedious. It must be remembered at this time that all shops closed at five o'clock and didn't open on Sundays. Nowadays, of course, anything goes.

My husband was oblivious to everything. He went to work all right, but he went out every night and was very selfish. On Saturday he sold cigarettes and ice-creams at Rotherham United's ground for a small Jewish man. Arnold received a 10% commission and did well, but he used all this as his pocket money when he went boozing. The savings I had for the house I was hoping to buy eventually disappeared, as he wanted a motorbike to travel to work on. Also, as he only had his demob suit, he needed another one, together with shirts and shoes. When I found myself pregnant, I also had to buy a pram, a cot, and other things for the baby. So after saving for all that time it came to nothing.

On 14th April 1947 our dear daughter Pauline Mary was born, weighing in at 6 lb 13 oz. The birth was no trouble at all as I was in very good shape. Sadly, Pauline was only a few months old when she developed whooping cough. It was terrible to watch her. At the same time my mother-in-law was rushed to hospital with gall stones, my father-in-law broke his ankle jumping out of a bus (he was a bus driver), and my husband came home with dermatitis from oil on the engine.

So there was just me to see to everything, including counting all the coupons for the shop and taking them to the food office — a very tedious job which I did on Thursday afternoons as it was half-day closing. My father-in-law was very good, looking after the baby while I did this chore. He loved his little grand-daughter and would have done anything for her. I then had to take the books up to the hospital for my mother-in-law to inspect, and by the time I went to bed at night I was exhausted. I was getting run down. They kept my mother-in-law in hospital for a week or two because they couldn't find out what was really wrong with her.

After a while, she sold the shop to a couple further down the street and moved into their rented terraced house. It was two-up two-down, with no bathroom and only a toilet at the bottom of the yard. One of the rooms had been partitioned into two very small bedrooms, nothing more than box-rooms. My mother-in-law had the big room, my father-in-law one of the box-rooms, and we had the remaining one. As it was only big enough for our bed and the cot, we had to climb over the bed to make it, and put our clothes in boxes under the bed. The landlady informed us that they didn't allow lodgers or sub-tenants, which was a blow, so I had to start looking around for somewhere to live. Notice it was "I" who had to do this; my husband was just not interested.

Firstly I went to the housing office to ask what our position was, and I was informed that we were way down the list because we only had one child. For many people, their husbands had only just come home from the war, and so they were having children like rabbits. We weren't sure where this left us as we didn't want to risk having any more children in the state we were in. We were also told that we would have to stay in Rotherham, because if we moved we would have our names taken off the housing list altogether.

We had already been on the list for six years, so I started touring around Rotherham. I walked for miles with my baby in the pram, but there wasn't a single room to be let anywhere. I went back to the housing office and explained the situation, but it made no difference. All they could suggest was to try the workhouse. I was flabbergasted — I told them that my husband had been fighting in India and Burma, but that made no difference, as there was a shortage of housing. It felt like being in a spider's web.

I wasn't going to be beaten, and so went back to our landlady and pleaded with her to bend the rules and let us stay until we could find somewhere. She was sympathetic and capitulated — yes, she'd let us stay. She told us that when the next house they had became vacant, then it was ours. I was elated. I went home and told Arnold and his parents, and they were so pleased. Mind you, I didn't know how long we had to wait.

In 1950 Grandma Overton died — that was Dad's mother. She lived in Nazareth House, Lancaster, which was a convent. She had to become a Catholic to get in. Her daughter, my Auntie Grace, was a Catholic, and that was the only way that they could get her in. The Mother Superior sent us word that she had died, and told us of the date of the funeral.

Ernest and Percy, Ernest's business partner, took us to the funeral in two small Ford cars — Mum and me in one, Dad and Arnold in the other. Mum had put some Army blankets in, and sandwiches as well — it's a good job she did. It wasn't a bad day when we set off, but when we got to the Yorkshire Moors, it was cloudy and bleak. We were going over the Snake Pass as it was the shortest route and there were no big roads in those days.

All of a sudden a snowstorm blew up, and you could hardly see a hand in front of you. It took us hours to get there — we crept all the way, as it was a narrow winding road with a sheer drop down one side. We kept as near to the safe side as possible, creeping along, and we managed to get to the other end of the road with a sigh of relief. One slip and we could have gone over the edge, the tension was terrible.

So we were late for the funeral — it was understandable, but not to Mother Superior! She told my dad off for being late, and Dad being polite told her what had happened. She couldn't have cared less. Dad wasn't bothered whether she was Mother Superior or

63

Queen Victoria — he put her in her place., and she didn't like it. She didn't offer us a cup of tea, but closed the door. So we got into the funeral car and went to the graveyard, and we came back frozen, stiff and hungry. We got into our cars and proceeded back home, stopping at the nearest town where Ernest treated us to a good lunch. We felt a lot better, and we took the longer route home, not over the Snake Pass, as we might not have been so lucky the second time! I'll never forget that day. Good Samaritans went to the bottom of the list with me.

After a few months I received a message from our landlady asking me to go and see her at her office. As I was walking through town I wondered if she had changed her mind and whether we would have to find somewhere else to live. As I went through the door she saw my face and said, "Don't worry Mrs Jackson, it's good news. We have a house coming empty and it's yours if you want it. It's only a two-up two-down terraced house, but it's in good condition near shops and schools. I'll let you know when it's ready for you." I couldn't believe my ears, and went home with my head in the clouds. However, the day the people were due to move out, they changed their minds. They were an Irish couple with six children in a two-bedroom house going into a three-bedroom council house with a bath. I couldn't believe it! Anyway, I don't know what went on between them, but they decided to flit the next day, and I was told to fetch the key which had been handed in.

Mum went with me to see the house because Arnold was working. I opened the door and we went in. The place was filthy and smelt terrible. After a few minutes Mum said, "Bugs, I'm afraid you have bugs." I was so disappointed, but she said, "Never mind, we'll soon get it into shape. At least you have a house at last. We'll go to the corporation and get the stovers in, and we'll soon get rid of them." So that's what we did, and it did the trick. Our next job was to strip the walls and scrub everything in sight. As we couldn't afford wallpaper, we used yellow wash as we had during the war. When our furniture arrived and we had sorted it out, it didn't look bad at all.

The next thing to do was get a job with a decent wage, and the only job like that was buffing. When the men came back from the war they wanted their jobs back, so Mum tipped up her job, crane-driving, and got a job buffing at Gordon Tools. She had been on this job for sometime when I joined her. I managed to get my daughter into a very good nursery. The government helped with the payments in those days, so I had no worries there. I lived in the Rotherham area but worked in Sheffield, so it took about an hour's travelling time.

Now we could get down to being a normal married couple — but, no, it was not to be. My husband still carried on as if he was a bachelor with no responsibilities. I dreaded the thought of buffing and doing all that dirty work, but we needed the money to decorate, and so out came the "mind over matter" that I had studied, and off I went.

Pauline was only about two years old when I had to put her in the nursery. I thought she would have cried, as there was a nurse called Peggy explaining to her that she couldn't take her dummy with her and she would have to hang it on this special peg with her name on it. She looked at the nurse with her big brown eyes and nodded shyly. "Bye-bye, love," I waved. "Bye-bye Mum, bye-bye Mum, bye-bye Mum." I had tears in my eyes. When I went to collect her I could hear nurse Peggy saying, "Pauline Jackson, you can just roll that toilet-roll up, and find your ribbon and sock before your Mum comes." When I looked round the corner my daughter was sitting on a little toilet trying to roll the toilet-roll (which was nearly up to her neck) back onto the cardboard centre. When she stood up she had one plait with a ribbon on and one without, one sock and shoe missing, and her knickers down around her ankles. That's what you get when you have a tomboy for a daughter! It helped to soften the first day at work.

I thought that we were managing nicely when the first blow fell. A knock came at the door, and there stood a small Jewish gentleman.

"Are you Mrs Jackson, Arnold's wife?"

"Yes, I am," I answered.

"Well, he works for me down at the football club."

"Oh, do come in," I said.

So he politely took his Homberg off and sat down. I gave him a cup of tea, and he started to talk.

"I'm afraid it's bad luck, Mrs Jackson. Arnold has not paid me any money for weeks; he has embezzled it"

It gave me such a shock that I turned pale and had to sit down.

"I'm so sorry," he said, "But if he doesn't pay me what he owes, I shall have to go to the police."

I pleaded, "Could you give me a few days and I'll try to get it for you."

He said that as I seemed a decent lady he'd give me the time. Then we shook hands and he left. My husband came home from work and I remonstrated with him about it. "Oh, you'll manage to get it love, I know you will," he replied in his most charming voice. I was thinking about our parents, knowing that any court case would make the papers, as this was so shocking in those days. So I went cap-in-hand to my dad. He had been working overtime and saving, especially while Mum was working. They were going to buy a public house for when the boys had finished their National Service. Dad lent the money to me with no questions asked, and I promised to pay him back one pound per week, which I did religiously — as he had taught us.

Dad left his job at the steel works in 1952 and he and Mum bought a pub, *The Crown*, known locally as "Low Drop", presumably because it was next to the big hammer at Arthur Lee's, the steel works. It was in Sheffield, and it was a beer house, which meant it sold no liquors or spirits, only beer. It was in the middle of a works area, and some of the men were working on the furnaces — they were allowed to drink beer while they were working, saying it was to "slacken the dust". I believe that it is a good old Yorkshire saying.

We thought that Dad had gone round the bend when we saw the dump — it was such a sorry place. Mind you, we all liked it after we had been there a while. It was a large turn-of-the-century pub, brass spittoons and all, which Mum got rid of immediately. When we checked the inventory we laughed at the articles that were included — it was like going back in time: two dozen spittoons, two dozen Punch and Judy doorstops made of iron, one Victorian whatnot in the corner of the stairs, and the star prize goes to the very large brass till on the counter. Every time you put money in it, it shot out and hit you in the stomach. In time we got used to it, and we jumped back out of the way.

Mum organised everything, and Dad and Peter did the barrels and cleaned the cellars. Barbara, John's wife, was a barmaid. They had a beautiful wedding, and the reception was held at the pub where there was plenty of room. There was a lovely big bar with stained glass shutters that came down, a snug room with a real fire, and a games room where the lads played dominoes and darts etc. My brother John helped at night, as he was working in the laboratories of the steel works. He and Barbara lived in a large bed-sit above the pub. I helped out in the day as I was between jobs, the work at Gordon Tools having dried up. Still, at least it meant that I could see Pauline to school and be there when she came home.

Mostly men came in to the pub, as there were no houses round about. They used to fetch beer by the gallon in those pot bottles which hillbillies used. We had to use a funnel to fill them.

This was the time that all of our family was together — my oldest brother Ernest with his wife Edith and their two boys, John and his wife Barbara, Peter, myself and my husband Arnold, and Mum and Dad. Later we didn't see Ernest very often as he had three businesses to attend to — a used car lot, a Washarama, and a music shop selling organs. Business people are always busy, that's how it goes.

One day, while emptying Arnold's jacket pockets to take his suit to the cleaners, out fell an opened letter. It was from one of his lady-friends.

At last here was some proof of his guilt. My heart pounded — I just couldn't believe that he had lied to my face and betrayed me after I had been so loyal to him, waiting all the time until he came home from overseas. I loved him. I went cold inside, I had never felt like this before. I could never get proof before this. This was a time, the late 1950s, when if anything like this happened, it was shocking. As I was on holiday, Pauline had gone shopping with her gran, so I washed and put some make-up on, had a cup of tea, and tried to keep calm. Still seething inside, I put my coat on and took the bus to Sheffield. As Arnold was at work, I had time on my hands. I read the lady's address from the top of the letter, asked a bus driver where the place was, and caught a bus there. I couldn't explain to anybody how I felt — it was just as if somebody had died, I felt bereaved.

I found the house and knocked on the door. A woman of about my age answered the door. "Are you Mrs Breeze?" I asked. She was, and looked me up and down. "Do you know Arnold Jackson rather well?" I continued.

"Ye-es," she stammered, going quite white. "Well, I'm Arnold's wife, do you mind if I come inside or do you want your neighbours to know?"

"Come inside, quick," she said ushering me into the house. We sat down and she made some tea. She was so shocked that she trembled — she thought I was going to strike her. I didn't though, and I had gone quite cold. I couldn't understand myself.

"Is that your husband?" I said, looking at a large picture of a naval officer on the sideboard. She nodded. "You shouldn't be going out with other people's husbands while he is away at sea. Would you like me to write and tell him what you're up to while he's away? He must have been home during the war."

She went a bit stroppy. "You can't because you don't know where he is."

"Oh, but I can soon find out," I said. "I've been in the Forces, I'll just get in touch with records." She went white again.

"Please don't," she pleaded. "He would stop my allowance at once, and I get a good one."

"Follow me on the next bus down to my house and I'll forget about it," I said, so she agreed.

Call it blackmail, or what you like, but I didn't care the mood I was in — I had been hurt terribly and didn't care. She did as she promised. I gave her a cup of tea and wasn't nasty as we chatted amiably.

The door latch went and Arnold came in. He couldn't see her because she was on the settee in front of the fire. This was the moment I was waiting for. "Arnold, you have a visitor." He turned round and saw her. He had such a shock — he lost his colour and was paralysed. He couldn't say anything for a moment or two, then all he said was, "What are you doing here?" He couldn't say much, as he was caught red-handed, and he hadn't time to find an excuse. This was the time he used to lie, but he couldn't do it, he was speechless.

After another cup of tea, I said, "You had better see this lady to the bus." I was still icy-calm. As soon as he left, I quickly packed his bag, put it outside, and bolted the door. When he came back he pleaded to be let back in, but I wouldn't — I put out the light and went to bed. So he slept in the toilet all night, then went down to his parents the next morning.

My mother-in-law came to see me to plead for Arnold — would I take him back, as he wouldn't be able to manage without me, as he still loved me a lot. She said that he was very sorry, and that he promised he wouldn't do it again. I refused at first, but I'm afraid that I didn't like upsetting her too much and we always respected each other; I agreed to have Arnold back. I never trusted him again, and I promised that if there was any more hanky-panky, he would definitely be out on his ear. How could he do that to me, keeping me short of money, while he took another woman out when I was working hard to keep us going . . . and paying his debts.

Everything went smoothly for a while, and then I had trouble with Arnold again — this time it was football tickets. I had to ask my husband's mother, and she said I could borrow the amount but that she would not give it to Arnold. I paid her a pound per week until she was repaid. One pound was a lot of money in those days, so it made us short every week.

Everything went smoothly again, until Arnold came in one day and announced that we were going to Rhodesia with the railway in Bulawayo. There was a house with the job and it was good money. I tried to discourage him, but he wasn't having any of it. I had misgivings. I would have to sell all the furniture I had bought while I was in the Air Force, and being second-hand I would hardly get anything for it. It was made of dark oak, and I had lovingly polished it and looked after it for years. We were waiting several months to see what happened when word came through that there was trouble with Ian Smith and his government, and there was an uprising in the copper mines. So the move was cancelled until further notice. How I breathed a sigh of relief!

However, things got worse. My husband started asking to borrow money again, but this time he didn't have his little jobs to fall back on. If I said "No", he would fly into a rage and try to borrow the rent money which was hidden under the staircarpet Once he punched me in the stomach, winding me, and another time he punched me in the jaw and my corner tooth nearly went through my top lip. I didn't cry, which I think he expected me to. I turned and faced him, and pointing a finger at him I said, "You won't do that again, I can promise you." He sneered.

Then one fateful Sunday Pauline went to visit her grandparents. We had had our tea when he came out saying, "Lend me some money, we're going to the railway club tonight." "No," was my answer. I saw his hand bunch up ready to strike me, but I was too quick for him. My left arm whipped round his neck and my right hand was on the back of his head. He was sitting down and I was standing behind his chair. He was helpless. All my feelings rushed over me — what a sensation. Why should I have to put up with this? I deserved more respect. I had tried my best for us, working hard to keep things going, but now that it had gone this far my personality and my confidence were going. Although I loved him, it didn't mean that I had to be the underdog — I had more intelligence than that. The worm had turned.

So I released the pressure slightly from around his neck and started talking. "I said you would not do that again, so the next time it will be curtains," squeezing his neck so my point would sink in. He was used to lying full length in front of the telly listening to John Arlott about cricket while I got the meals ready, expecting everything to be passed to him. "You will not put the telly on and close the curtains all the time, or I'll take the television to the bottom of the garden and smash it against the wall." I squeezed again. "We are not going to Rhodesia, or anywhere else." Squeeze. "And finally, ask for any more rent money and you'll get it right enough — that, the rent book, and several other articles right up your gear box. Got it?" He tried to nod but he couldn't. I took my arm away quickly, but he didn't move as he was still trying to catch his breath.

I went upstairs, locked the door and sat on the bed, waiting for the retaliation. He came upstairs and knocked on the door. "Joan, love, come downstairs, I'll not do that again." I waited a few minutes, then I went downstairs expecting something to happen. But it didn't. He was quietly sitting down.

"Joan, you could have killed me doing that."

"I know," I replied. "Weren't you lucky I was taught when to stop? Mind you, I still know a few more tricks like that I can use." I can honestly say he altered in his ways towards me after this.

It was about this time that I went back to buffing at Gordon Tools. I wasn't exactly looking forward to it, but the money was reasonable.

For several years everything was normal — well, almost. Then one morning Arnold came back from work after being on nights. His breakfast was in the oven, and Mum had come across to go to work with me. He came and put his arm around my shoulders, kissed me and said, "Be careful love, there's thick fog on the line." We went to work, but by the time it reached dinner, the cold I had suspected that I had was developing. I was perspiring and sneezing so much that my boss called the works van and took me home. Mum was going to follow after she finished her work.

I opened the door and went in, but I had a strange feeling that the house was empty. There on the table was a note. I picked it up and read it. "Joan, I'm leaving. You are too good for me." Though it was Friday Arnold hadn't left any housekeeping money, although it didn't amount to much when he did — that's why I had to go out to work. When I went across to tell Mum and Dad, they couldn't believe it.

On a happier note, Peter married Deirdre in 1956.

After Arnold left in 1959 I couldn't eat properly, and I wasn't able to go buffing again because it was dangerous — you could take your fingers off if you weren't alert. I don't think that people realised the danger that we were in all the time. As we nearly all had long hair, we had to keep it wrapped up in a scarf. One of our girls was scalped as she hadn't wrapped her hair up properly — a hank of hair fell down and got trapped in the high-powered spindle. I had two stitches in my right hand near my little finger as one of the girls had tripped and caught my elbow. My hand caught the glazer, and as mine was like a fine grinding wheel, in a split-second you could see the bare knuckle underneath. Out came the car and I was rushed to the top of the street to the casualty ward of the Royal Hospital.

Sally, who worked beside Mum, already had two fingers missing on her right hand. One day she had turned to Mum and said, "May, have you got your white towel on you?" Mum said, "Yes, why Sally?" Sally answered, "Pick up my finger from the floor will you? I shall have to take it up to the hospital with me." The car came and within a few minutes they had whizzed her up to the hospital and were stitching the finger back on. Those women were tough and kind-hearted. At first I never thought that I would stay in that job, but I did as I had to survive and the money wasn't too bad at that time. However, after the trauma of being deserted by

Arnold, I couldn't concentrate, and I lost three stones in no time at all.

I managed to get a part-time job as a cook in a transport cafe for Mrs Fox. The wages were only £3 a week plus a free meal, but I never had time to eat it properly as we were always so busy. I went to the doctor's for a tonic, but when he examined me he said I was badly underweight. If I didn't put any weight on by the time I went back, I would be sent to hospital.

Anyway, the following week I went back and after weighing me he said, "You haven't gained an ounce, Mrs Jackson, but you haven't lost any either, so you'll be all right. If you wait until after the surgery, I'll give you a bit of advice." So I waited, wondering what advice it would be. He told me how to do deep relaxation, only they didn't call it that then. He said it would be very hard to do but that I should persevere, so I did. Every so often I went to the doctor's for a check-up. He would ask me how I was progressing, and I told him I was mastering it all right. He was pleased. That advice has lasted me up until this day, and I have a lot to thank him for.

Now Mrs Fox was a character. She was a big woman, 22 stone and nearly 6 feet tall, twice the size of me. I was only 5 foot 3 inches and 7 stone in weight. Mrs Fox worked in the cafe side, dishing dinners out and taking money, I cooked in the kitchen. The cafe was very popular and always busy. This work was the only job I could get that was part-time in 1959. Why did I always get these terribly hard jobs? One day my prince would come, with a glass slipper for me, and we would fall in love and live happily ever after — well, I could dream, couldn't I? I never thought it would ever happen.

Mrs Fox would have made a good sergeant major — the only thing was that I was rebellious, and I would still say what I wanted. If I was sacked I could always get another horrible job that nobody wanted, there were plenty of those about. However, Mrs Fox liked me (she was getting value for money), and although I should have started work at 9.30a.m., at 8.00 o'clock she would shout through the letter box in broad Yorkshire, "Joan, a' tha' up, we're going to a house, they're going abroad." That meant that we were going to buy somebody's furniture and crockery cheap as she was paying cash, and they wanted a quick sale. She would ask me the value, I would nod my head, and then she would buy. The things she bought would have shaken some people — garden sheds, sewing machines, curtains (good ones, as these were residential homes), caravan cookers, and pots and pans were thrown in for nothing with lovely furniture. "A' thee tecking notice, lass?" she asked. Looking at me now, I must have been, because I could have sold snow to the Eskimos later on.

The Irish navvies that we had boarding with us came in very handy as they had a small van which they went round in, collecting all these items. They put them in two garages in the large yard at the back of the cafe. After three o'clock people would come to buy them. It fascinated me as Mrs Fox never parted with hard cash, she always traded. The lads had a free holiday in the four prefabs that she bought when the corporation was dismantling them. One young man did the plumbing, one the wiring, and two decorated and painted them — she would do their laundry and give them free meals. Everybody was satisfied with this arrangement.

I remember that one day a bunch of reps came in whom Mrs Fox knew as they had been in before. Their firm paid for their meals and one paid for them all from their kitty. Mrs Fox had gone into the kitchen, the reps were leaving, and the man with the money was going out without paying. Mrs Fox had come back quicker than he thought, she grabbed him by the scruff of the neck and yanked him back into the shop. To my surprise she turned him upside down and shook him, and his wallet and money all fell on the floor as she shouted, "Joan, pick up the money for the six dinners and 10/- for the trouble we've had." Turning to the young man she said, "Don't ever come in here again." He scuttled out of the door as she had a voice to match her size. It was like tangling with Peggy Mount, the actress.

The next man who tried going out of the door without paying was a little Irish fellow with a cowboy hat. He walked out without paying his lodging money. Mrs Fox took his large case off him, leaving him only with the clothes that he stood up in. She wouldn't part with his case until he brought the money. He fetched a policeman, but it didn't make any difference, he still didn't get the case back. He finally brought the money and he got his case back, so all's well that ends well, as usual.

Bill Fox, Mrs Fox's second husband, was a miner. Everyday before he went to work, or when he came back, he rumbled the potatoes and eyed them for the next day. He was a very nice man, laid back and very easy to get on with. Mrs Fox had bought a chalet in a lovely spot overlooking a reservoir. When Bill was on holiday he would go up there picking bilberries for pies in the cafe. We went up there one day to see how he was getting on, when he was sorting them out into white pails. He asked me to have a look, and he showed me a small well with a natural spring of crystal clear water running through it. I tasted it and it was like nectar; I hadn't tasted water like that since I was a child. Further down there was a hollow filled with water in which there was a net full of cans of beer. Bill had a wireless and racing papers, and he insisted that he never got bored as this was his little heaven with peace and quiet and everything he needed. I thought that it must be peaceful without Mrs Fox's booming voice rumbling past him everyday. She looked after him well, and he was a happy man.

Mrs Fox's first husband had been killed down the pit, and she had four small children under five to bring up. They were all grown up and married when I started working for her, and Bill got on very well with them and loved them all.

Before I finished working for Mrs Fox I did her income tax, her books for the accountant, and several other small jobs. She used to put all her bills and receipts in a large drawer. They would be sticky with custard and jam, so I used to have a damp cloth and wipe them clean first, then get a piece of string with a bodkin at one end and a large button at the other to thread the bills onto it and tie them up so that Mrs Fox didn't mix them up again! The accountant was intrigued."Who is doing your books, Mrs Fox?" She told him it was Joan, her cook. "Well, you want to hold onto her, Mrs Fox, she's got a good idea there," he said.

Another time, when we had finished, she took me to see a gypsy fortune-teller called Tillie. "I don't believe in that rubbish," I said, "Besides, I haven't the money to waste on things like that" It cost half-a-crown, but Mrs Fox paid for it, so I couldn't get out of it. We called in at Mum's to tell her I would be a bit late, and she said the same as me. Arriving at Tillie's we knocked on the front door — it was a dark winter's evening, with only a gaslight fixed on the wall, making it look very eerie. She opened the door a bit and said, "Rozzers?" It's a good job that Mrs Fox knew what that meant, because I didn't. "No, we're not police," Mrs Fox answered, "someone recommended you." Tillie opened the door and let us in.

She gave us a cup of tea, then she sat up in bed and we sat on chairs beside her. Mrs Fox went first, and Tillie said, "Your friend there is going to leave you and get a job." "No she isn't, are you?" asked Mrs Fox. I had been thinking about changing jobs and had told Mum as we were having a right job making ends meet. Tillie also told her that she would be going into hospital and I would run the business for her. "No, I'm not," said Mrs Fox. "Yes, you are, whether you like it or not, and stop arguing," said Tillie sharply. "I don't know

80

what sort of business it is, but she's going to run it for you."

Then she turned to me. "Oh! Trouble, lots of trouble, I see a broken wedding ring that means your husband is going to leave you or he has left you already. Don't turn your back or trust him, he's no good for you, he never has been." I couldn't believe what I was hearing. "You are going to have an awful time of it, but never mind lass, you'll come through it in the end."

Anyway, a couple of weeks later Mrs Fox was forced to go into hospital for an operation. Of course I was in charge of the cafe, with the help of Mrs Fox's friend from the village, Mrs Green, who used to live in. She was middle-aged and a good worker, and we got on well together. One day halfway through cooking the dinner the gasman came to cut off the gas.

"What are we going to do?" Mrs Green said. "Watch this and follow me," I said. "Would you like your dinner while you're here? It's almost ready — on the house of course." I said to the man.

"There's steak, lamb chops, pork chops, or steak and kidney pie with vegetables and Yorkshire puddings, then rice pudding or bilberry pie or jam roly-poly and custard, with tea or coffee."

He chose steak and rice pudding. I told him to take his time as I sat him at a table in the corner out of the way, and I gave him the daily paper. I bet he thought it was his birthday. Mrs Green said that she would have never thought of doing that. Later on I took the money that was owing out of the till, and paid him. "Thanks, that was the best dinner I've had for a long time," he said.

It was all organic in those days. We didn't have a freezer so everything was fresh, and I used to fetch the meat in as I came to work. Mrs Fox told me to tell the butchers that she would pay them at the weekend. She knew what she was doing. As both the butchers knew I was divorced and single, they were both vying for my affections, so I got the best steak and chops, and they cut the steak and kidney up for me. Unfortunately for them I was trying to find myself, not get tangled-up again.

Mum and Dad helped me back to health, but it took me up to two years to do it. Then one day Dad said, "Pidge, wouldn't you like a proper career, instead of playing about on those odd jobs?"

"I would love it, Dad, but what could I do? I'm 36 now."

"Try the Air Force, love, you have experience and an excellent reference. We'll bring our Pauline up for you," he said. Mum and Dad were in their early 60s at the time, and had sold the pub and were living in a small pre-fab. Dad was working as a labourer for the corporation.

So I went to the recruiting place in Sheffield once again. I explained my situation, and the recruiting officer said that they took recruits with experience up to the age of 39. I would only need a refresher course and then I would be on the jets. He gave me forms to fill in. So I completed them and put them on the sideboard, ready to hand in. They were there for a few days until I could get up to Sheffield again, but before I could go, fate took a nasty turn.

Dad was brought home from work ill. He was taken to hospital for tests, and when they came through he was diagnosed as having lung cancer. I knew I couldn't go into the Air Force now, so I tore up the papers, and shut my mind off things. I wasn't bitter — I had taught myself that whatever was thrown at me I should not be disappointed.

We lost Dad six months later, and besides losing a father I lost a friend. He had taught me a lot through my life and he used to say, "Keep going, Pidge, it doesn't matter what happens."

On My Own

Now we were all right, weren't we? Mum was on her own and I was on my own, and we had about £5 between us to pay two rents and keep three of us. I had to find a way out, so I wrote to Gordon Tools, asking if they had any vacancies. "Certainly, start as soon as possible, and bring your mother, we're short of buffers." So I got in touch and explained the situation, that I couldn't let Mrs Fox down, but that Mum would start again straight away.

Fortunately, Mrs Fox was better again when I broke the news that I had been looking for another job and was going back to buffing. She had a fit, saying, "I thought you were happy here, Joan." I tried to tell her that I needed more money to live on, that our Pauline was growing up, and that she could eat like a horse. It didn't click, and she wasn't forthcoming with any more cash. I told her that I wouldn't leave her in the lurch. I would wait until she had managed to get another cook.

Mrs Fox now said that she was going to sell the business; she put it on the market, and someone came to see it almost immediately. It was an elderly Italian lady with two sons, and I think that they wanted to turn it into an Italian restaurant. The woman watched me baking, and said to me in broken English, "You good cook, very quick, will you work for me? I double your pay." Mrs Fox heard this and said, "I've changed my mind." The woman was so disappointed. "I could have offered you double," Mrs Fox said. I didn't answer, and thought to myself, "Then why didn't you?" Anyway, some young women turned up for the job and she picked two that she thought were suitable. When I was showing them what to do in the kitchen, one of the girls asked me if I did all that on my own. I told her that I did, and she said, "I wonder why Mrs Fox has picked two of us?" I was wondering that myself; she must have something in mind.

When I arrived home my daughter and I looked at the expensive bowl of pot flowers that Mrs Fox had bought me. We laughed, and Pauline said, "Mum, do you remember when Mrs Fox bought you that? You weren't very enthusiastic when she gave it to you."

"I should think not," I replied, "because when you are starving you can't eat pot flowers. If Mrs Fox had given me a pound extra instead, I would have been most grateful."

She bought me that for looking after the business for a fortnight while she was in hospital. A few days later a flower fell off without anyone touching it, and Pauline joked that it must have heard me. I never did stick the flower back on, I couldn't bring myself to do it. I still have it after all these years, and when I look at it, it brings me back down to earth and keeps me from being smug.

I remember that when we went back buffing we were a bit better off and were welcomed with open arms. However, the money wasn't all that good. This was in 1961, but they were still paying the same as 1948 when we first started there. Anyway, we couldn't do anything else except go back, as Mum would not have got a job anywhere else at 62. We were experienced and on piecework, so we managed.

In order to get a bit of extra money coming in Mum and I pooled our talents. I could sew, do alterations, make dresses and loose covers, paint lampshades and make pottery — there wasn't much I couldn't do. Mum could crochet, make matinee coats, bonnets, shawls etc. So we did that at nights while watching television.

I remember that things were so tight at Christmas that whilst Pauline was with Grandma Jackson for the day, Mum and I shared a pork chop and a bottle of milk stout between us for Christmas dinner. Things may have been tough, but we were satisfied with what we had got.

We finished paying for the four-berth caravan Dad had started buying before he died. We used to let it out to pay the ground rent and bus fares so that we could go at weekends. We enjoyed our days there on the sand dunes at Mablethorpe. It helped us forget our worries when we were there. When we made our final payment it was like winning the pools — we celebrated with a glass of milk stout and a pork sandwich each. It was ours at last after struggling to pay for it over such a long time, and so we were a bit better off.

One year, at the end of September, Mum took Pauline to the caravan for a week to close it for the winter. I was at a loose end with them both being away, so I went to Sheffield to do a bit of window-shopping and to go and see my brother who had a car business. When I arrived Ernest was stood talking to a man. I thought that he looked nice, but he was probably married. Why did I think that? I had been on my own for nearly five years and men didn't interest me. There were plenty of nice young men interested, but I said "No." I wanted to find myself again.

My brother introduced me to Albert Belk. We started talking, and even when Ernest was called away we carried on talking. Albert eventually took me to the bus stop, and then asked me if I would like to go to the new cinema that had opened and see *El Cid*. So we made a date for the next day. When I arrived home I just couldn't believe what I had done. Going out with a man, well, it wasn't like me was it? Anyway, there was something about him that I liked. He wasn't much bigger than me; not what you would call handsome, but he was cuddly. This was in stark contrast to Arnold who was six feet tall and good looking, with a good build, being a sportsman.

I think Fate smiled on me that day. When Mum came home, I told her about Albert and she was highly delighted. Mum said she was glad, as she thought I was getting a right old maid and that I was going to be a man-hater for the rest of my life.

I was still a bit cautious. I didn't tell Albert my address — he lived in Sheffield and I lived in

Rotherham. One night I was on my own, doing some sewing, when there was a knock at the front door. There was no expectation of anyone attacking in those days, so you didn't have to be careful like you do now, and I went to see who it was. There was Albert with a sheepskin rug rolled up under his arm, a present for me, and the first present I had had in years. I thought it was marvellous and Albert looked pleased to see me.

"Come in, Albert," I said. "How did you find me? I didn't give you my address."

"I did a bit of sleuthing," he answered. "I found the park you mentioned, and asked a couple if they knew Joan Jackson who did sewing and alterations. They said everybody knew you around here." They must have been my customers.

Anyway, I made him comfortable and gave him some tea and biscuits, and then we talked and talked. Believe it or not, this was the start of something big. We found that we had a lot in common and shared the same sense of humour. It was lovely to talk to somebody who understood what I was on about. My first husband only knew four subjects — money, sport, drinking and womanising, so I had always been limited to what I could talk to him about. Anything deeper than these and he was stymied. Albert and I started to see each other regularly, and one night after the pictures he asked if I would be his girl. I told him that I thought I was, to which he replied, "Oh, did you? — that's lovely."

When it was near my birthday, Albert asked, "Joan, would you like to get engaged?"

I simply said, "All right Albert." This was only six weeks after we had met. Then he asked Pauline what she thought, and she said, "That would be lovely, Albert." Then we went across to Mum's. Would she give her blessing?

"Yes, Albert, but you had no need to ask me, you're both adults."

"Yes, Ma, but we are all involved you know. I'm joining your family."

She was over the moon. "Oh," she said, "Somebody with nice manners, isn't it lovely to be asked?"

Albert was a pattern-maker, and when he told me initially, I thought that this meant he was a tailor. He soon put me right — he made patterns in wood as moulds for precision machinery. The metal was shaped in these intricate moulds. Albert was a master craftsman, and had served a seven-year apprenticeship. He loved his work and was highly skilled.

A fortnight before Albert and I were married, Mrs Fox turned up just as we were having tea. She knocked at the door and walked straight in. She took a look at Albert and introduced herself, as I had written to her and told her that I was getting married.

"Joan, I have a job for you, a good one. I've bought a fish and chip restaurant at Cleethorpes, on the same site as where the pre-fabs are. It has a field at the back, where we have caravans to let, and there's a large flat over the top. I want you to run it for me."

I thought to myself, "What, on the same £3 per week plus a free dinner, no thanks!"

Albert said, "Sorry, Mrs Fox, but Joan and I are getting married in a fortnight's time, and I have a decent job. I'm going to look after her well from now on, it's time she had a bit of peace and quiet so that she can please herself and do what she wants to do."

This sounded lovely, as I hadn't had anyone to look after me for years, and it seemed my luck had changed at last. Mrs Fox went away dejected, but she didn't fall out with me, and she sent us a pair of hand-embroidered pillows made in Madeira as a wedding present. They had flowers all over them, and none fell off! At Christmas we exchanged cards, and hers was always a special one, as she had been a friend, sort of. When I had all my troubles while I worked for her, my mind would wander at times, thinking how to put arsenic in her tea at elevenses, and it did take my mind off my troubles!

Albert and I were married about five months after first meeting, and Mum gave me away. I had already met Albert's relations, and they had all taken to me and I to them. I couldn't understand it, everything had gone so smoothly. As a rule, if I wanted anything, a large lump of bad luck was thrown at me and I didn't get whatever it was. This luck lasted with me for 38 years. It seemed that when I changed my name the luck changed for the better. I was now like Midas, everything I touched turned to gold.

I was still buffing, but Albert didn't stop me, saying he'd always let me do what I wanted to — he understood me. A few weeks later I left buffing and got a job as a part-time cook in an insurance company.

Mum was still buffing and I was so sorry to leave. We had made so many friends, real friends who helped one another, laughing and singing (and swearing) together to forget our worries. By the way, I still didn't swear. Although I was the one who said I would never do buffing, I had been doing it for ten years on and off.

My life with Albert was very good — we were best friends, as well as husband and wife, and we had a lot in common, like reading. I read classics and everything that was interesting, including psychic matters, mind over matter, and body language. Albert read the same kind of books, but his favourites were autobiographies. We were always discussing things between us, and we communicated very well, which was lovely, as I couldn't with my first husband Arnold. He thought that I was bonkers because I liked art, good music and reading. He called all this rubbish, so we didn't discuss much. I kept quiet and agreed as much as I could with him, to keep the cart on the wheels, as the old saying goes. My personality was slipping away, we weren't suited at all. We were too young to get married.

Albert and I had great respect for each other, and helped one another with everything. One of the main things we had was trust, and we were straightforward with one another, which meant a lot to us. Albert was also very good with my daughter Pauline, and she had great respect for him. She called him "Albert" to his face, but "Dad" when talking to anybody about him. She could never understand how two men could be so opposite.

Albert was gentle, understanding, loving and very generous. He was so proud of me, and helped me in anything I did, giving me confidence. He also had a lovely sense of humour. For 38 wonderful years we were friends as well as being equals — this makes a big difference, as when you are both together without children, you can communicate about things.

"Joan Belk"

After three years of being married to Albert, he said to me, "Joan love, wouldn't you like to do something interesting for a change?" It reminded me of Dad; he had asked me the same question, only in a different way.

"Yes, I would love to, I'd like a nice little café somewhere."

"Then you shall have one," he said. It took me by surprise.

Anyway, Pauline and I went to look at cafés, but none suited, so I ended up with an empty shop on a rough estate as I'd had another idea by this time. Mum and Pauline thought that I had taken leave of my senses. The shop was filthy and had been a cake shop, and the previous owner had also roasted chickens in it. It had been empty for some time, so there were plenty of cobwebs. It took me about three weeks to clean and paint it inside and out, but it looked great when it was finished. I papered the back wall with a good washable paper decorated with golliwogs and toys. The two large counters were painted black with red linoleum tops, and everything else was painted white. The outside was black and white, with my name "Joan Belk" over the window.

I looked up with pride. Now it was up to me to make a go of it. Albert helped me out by making all the shelves, and then said that I needed some money for my stock — he was offering to give me whatever I wanted.

"No, Albert, I want to borrow £300, but I need to do this myself."

That was for the lease and for some stock, as I had £100 of my own, and I wanted to see what I could achieve with that.

"OK love, you know what you are doing," Albert replied.

So while I was waiting for the lease to come through I bought some material from the market and started dressmaking. I made children's dresses and rompers. As it was the 1960s there were some lovely designs. I opened the shop just before Whitsun and sold them all. I started off with wool and baby linen, and listened to what customers wanted and bought it in if I thought it would sell. When the shop was not busy I did clothes alterations, which brought customers in as well. Albert bought me a present for the opening — well, it was actually two presents, a sewing machine and an iron and ironing board. They were very handy and couldn't have been better presents.

I must have looked a soft touch, because first one person and then another tried to borrow money, but I said I was sorry but that I didn't lend money. I meant it, and they soon got the message and stopped asking. I didn't give credit at all — I would lay things by for them, but they didn't get the goods until they had paid for them. One customer came in and she asked me if I'd been a buffer, as she had been one for years. It took one buffer to know another, it was instinct — even now I can still tell a buffer. Anyway, word must have got round, and I never had any trouble from anyone. I must explain that this was one of the roughest estates in Sheffield. Nearly everyday there was something interesting happening.

I ploughed everything back into the business for two years, and then I was able to take a wage out of it. This was handy as Albert's firm came out on strike for nine months, but we managed by pulling together. Eventually we got back to normal. The shop was doing well as I was selling plenty of wool and Marks and Spencer's seconds. I'd put them in a large cardboard box marked "Seconds" with a price on it, and then stand back and wait. Every Friday it was like a bun-fight when the warehouse delivered the stock. I used to sell anything and everything that was a bargain, giving value for money. I had the customers' trust so I did well.

One day, a friend of ours, Colin, came in to tell me that he was working at a factory that made men's underwear — pants and vests. I had an idea.

"Have they any pants with short legs?" He looked puzzled.

"Yes, as many as you want, but they are seconds."

"Smashing," I said, and ordered a large quantity. He brought them and put them in a box on the counter.

95

They were cheap to me, so I sold them cheaply and gave Colin some money, and so we were all satisfied. I wrote on the box, "Suitable for incontinence". Well, they went like wildfire. The customers were fetching two or three sets at a time. One woman told me that it was a God-send, and she kept taking them up to her husband in hospital as he was incontinent and pants rotted very quickly, so it had been getting expensive.

After leaving school, Pauline worked in the warehouse at Gordon Tools where Mum was still a buffer. She then decided that she wanted to be a cook, and while working at the YMCA met Bill St Clair. They married when she was 19 and soon afterwards had Mark, my special grandson, who was born on 3rd June, my dad's birthday. Pauline and Bill were together seven years before they parted, which was strange because they are still the best of friends.

My next bright idea came one day when Pauline came to help. As she was a single parent she was short of money and she also needed to get away from things. I knew, I'd been there.

"We'll have a holiday," I said to Albert, "and I have a bright idea how to get the money, love."

"Have you," he asked, "What is it, my dear?"

He was used to this, and it got to be a joke with us.

"Albert, do you know where I can get a gross of Durex from?" His eyebrows shot up and he smiled.

"And what are you going to do with a gross of Durex?"

"Leave it to me," I said.

96

"Well, I know where to get them, there's a place in town that supplies chemists," he replied.

The next day Albert trotted down town and came back with a box under his arm. "You've got a discount on them as you are trade — aren't you the lucky one?" He still didn't ask me what I was going to do with them, he just smiled. Curiosity would have killed me! I had put an advert in the *Rotherham Advertiser*, "Durex 4 Pkts 10/- under plain wrapper, first class stamp, swift delivery," together with my address. There it was in print, very nice. I asked Pauline to fetch me a bundle of brown envelopes of a certain size and about 50 first-class stamps, and then we waited for Monday morning. Don't forget we had a good postal service in those days.

Monday morning came, and so did the postman.

He emptied nearly half a bag of envelopes. "Somebody's birthday, Joan?"

"No," I answered, "Just business."

We looked at the pile in amazement and we were very excited.

"Get cracking, Pauline, one at a time, and put them in this box."

As we emptied them, out came ten-shilling notes and pound notes and addresses. So we got to work, and we had them all ready before dinnertime for the post, so that they would be received the next morning. You could call this mail-order, I suppose. This became a routine, a few coming in during the week but the bulk coming in on Monday mornings. As business was a bit slack on Mondays it was ideal for us. This went on for a long time, and we had several enjoyable holidays in Torquay over the years; we had earned them. Every so often I used to get a bright idea and Albert backed me every inch of the way. I had never had such freedom to use my brain.

I gave my daughter a few words of wisdom: "You have to get your customers' confidence, have a routine, and be civil and polite. It doesn't matter how you feel or who they are," and we had some really tough customers where we were in that district.

One day one of my customers came in and asked me if I bought Green Shield stamp books as she was skint. I used to give the stamps with purchases, and the customers loved them. "Yes," I said, "I'll give you ten shillings for a clean and full book." Other shops were paying seven and sixpence, and that two and sixpence made all the difference. The customers rolled in with them. They were buying things such as wool etc, so I was getting more custom.

A friend of Albert's from work, Stan Charles, came to our house one night to visit and asked me if I could get him some Green Shield books.

"How many do you want, Stan?" I asked.

"A lot," he said. He was a scoutmaster and the scouts were buying canoes and sports gear.

"Well, I've got a lot, and being the scouts I'll let you have them at twelve shillings per book. I've paid ten bob each for them." He couldn't believe his luck and he was highly delighted. He was happy, the scouts were happy, and I was happy — after all, we were shifting hundreds of books. I know it wasn't a lot, but two shillings meant something in those days. I only had to count them and hand them over, so everyone was happy.

Finally the last idea came. "Albert, how much silver is there in our coinage?"

He answered, "I don't know, how much silver *is* there in our coinage?"

"No, I'm not telling you, I'm asking you."

"Well, I know so many are all silver and some have nickel in them. Get a book out of the library, you might be able to find out there. What's this brilliant idea you've got now?"

"Well, we are going to change to decimal coinage, aren't we? That means that there will be a tremendous amount of obsolete silver knocking about, and somebody will be buying it to melt it down, so I'm going to start collecting it as from now."

He shook his head. "Joan, I'd love to know where you get all these ideas from?"

"My dear old Dad," I answered. "He used to say to me, you have to grab every opportunity you can if it's good, and be a positive thinker. He was a miner, and he sold tons of chocolates and plain toffees and chewing gum down the pit where he worked, because the miners couldn't smoke down there. How was that for an idea?"

"I know where you get it from now," he smiled. So it began. Every pre-1947 silver coin in the till I exchanged for new money. It took a long time to change, and I kept taking little bags of them home. Towards the end they became scarce. In the paper I saw that twice the value for old silver coins was being given. Ah, it had started! I showed Albert, and he smiled and said, "So you were right love, weren't you?" I was patient and waited. A week or two passed. Three times the value came next. "Are you selling, love?" "Not yet, Albert." I waited. Then it came, four times — that was it. I sent for the man to come, and he paid me there and then. £2,400 for £600 of coins I had saved. My husband was flabbergasted.

"You'll soon be a millionaire at this rate. What I'd like to know is how do you know when to sell?"

"Before you get to the top. You don't have to wait until you hit the jackpot and be greedy." This kept me in good stead later on in life.

Then one night after tea, Albert asked, "Have you had a good day, love?"

I answered, "Yes, very good, that's why I'm going to sell the shop." I had owned it for nine years.

"But you're doing so well love, why are you selling?"

"Because that's when you should sell, when it's doing well, and besides, as I can't expand and I've reached the limit — I want a change."

So the shop was put up for sale. The first person who came to see it bought it. She was one of my customers who had had her eye on my little business for years, and she was thrilled to death. Anyway, we had to wait for things to be transferred, so I showed her the ropes and she got used to it. I warned her of the pit-falls — one was not to give credit.

I paid my taxes, capital gains, etc, and then I packed my personal things and handed everything over to the new owner. Pauline and I walked up the street hand-in-hand, and she said, "Turn and have a last look at your little shop, it was your hobby and you made it what it was." The tears were streaming down her face.

"No, Pauline, you should never look back and regret things, you look forward to the next project" She squeezed my hand, and smiling through her tears she nodded. We had had such fun in that little shop.

When I arrived home my husband had the tea ready and he smiled at me.

"Have you retired now, love?"

"For the present," I said. That present lasted less than a month.

The Bank

Only a few weeks after selling the shop, I said to Albert, "I'll have to go to work again, I'm getting bored."

"All right, love, you do what you want to, so long as you're happy, but you're going to have a struggle getting another job at fifty."

"We'll see," I replied.

I had all day to hunt as Albert was at work and I was on my own. The first two turned me down as they didn't take on people over 40. This made me even more keen, as I am a determined type! That week I ended up with four opportunities: one in a silversmiths and cutlers, which I had experience in; the magistrates' court making refreshments in the intervals; thirdly, a test to go for audio-typing at Stannington College; and finally, I had been to the labour exchange, and saw an advert for a toilet attendant at the Midland Bank clearing centre that had just been built. I made up my mind, and the bank won. I applied by letter and received an interview almost immediately. I told the family and they thought that I'd flipped my lid. "Toilets?" they kept saying, "Toilets?" I replied that it didn't matter, and I was sure that this was it. It was. I went for an interview, as did forty-odd other women. I went soberly dressed but still in fashion, with a black leather coat with a fur collar (they were still in vogue in the 1970s!), nice black leather shoes, a white polo-neck sweater and a good leather handbag. One flashy young thing opposite me said, "Why are you applying. You're too old." Cheeky. I just looked at her and said, "Think so?" and gave her one of my nicest smiles. This was my psychology, and she looked baffled. This is how I like it. I used to look quiet and so people underestimated me, giving me the upper-hand. It happens to this day, although now I look like somebody's little white-haired old granny, but inside I'm still dynamite and love to see the look on some people's faces.

Anyway, I got the job. When the person who interviewed me asked if there were any questions, I said yes. Why had she picked me out of all those young ladies, especially as some would have needed the money more than me. She smiled and said, "Things don't work like that at a bank — you are straightforward, disciplined because you've been in the services, you looked me straight in the eyes and you didn't twitter." A thought went through my head that it was just the toilets, but she must have read my mind.

"No, Mrs Belk, it is not just the toilets, you could get promoted in due course and you never know what's around the corner," and she proved to be right. They wanted to know everything about me: did I have a police record, where had I worked before, had I been self-employed, what sort of business had I worked in, and if I had gone bankrupt.

"No, it was a lucrative small business which I had sold while it was doing well." Brother, it was like getting into M15.

I had to go to their doctor for a full examination. He was fascinated by my deep breathing, in, out, in, out; I thought he was never going to stop. He said that if everybody did that, there wouldn't be so much illness floating about. He asked me how long I had been doing deep-breathing exercises, and he smiled and nodded approval when I told him that I had been doing the exercises together with meditation for a good few years. I was in.

I reported to the bank on 5th April 1976. There was only one floor open. I went into the foyer and asked for the head messenger, who was very pleased to see me and introduced me to the rest of the lads (messengers), about 25 of them. They showed me where things were. The bank had given me a conference room on the ground floor. There was everything I needed in this room — stacks of toilet rolls, roller towels, soaps, nail brushes and drinking cups. There was a row of easy chairs, a large table, mugs, kettle and telephone. Peter the head messenger came in and gave me instructions.

"Have you bought your knitting and a book to read, Joan, as there's only the seventh floor open? Do the job right, Joan, and nobody will breath down your neck and you'll be your own boss."

I couldn't believe my luck. I worked at the bank for nearly 17 years, and I never did have anyone breathing down my neck, as I was always conscientious.

I took my coat off, hung it in the locker they had given me, and then went up to the seventh floor. After seeing that everything was in order I went down to my room. There I sat mesmerised: such luxury — so this was how the bank worked. My mind went back to when I was buffing. We didn't even have a bar of soap to wash our filthy hands with, and at dinner time we had to wrap the bottom part of our sandwich in paper before we could eat it, sitting on oil drums filled with spanners round a potbellied stove — unbelievable! Break time came, and the lads trooped in.

"Do you mind us coming in here for our break, as we don't like to see you on your own?"

"No," I replied. "It'll break the day up."

So that's how it was. The lads would come in, have a smoke and a cup of tea or coffee and a chat.

They were moving in furniture that had come up from London and so they were ready for a cuppa. We got on like a house on fire, and I still had my sense of humour from being a buffer which never changed. Having been in the Forces, I was one of them as most of them had been in the Forces as well, so we had a good rapport between us that lasted for twelve months.

Then one day I was sent for by the head of all the messengers from across the road. Off I trotted, thinking to myself, "I wonder what he wants me for — I wonder whether it's something to do with their toilets?" No, it wasn't."

"Do sit down, Mrs Belk, I have a proposition to put to you." I couldn't think what that could be. Anyway, he went on, "You like a challenge Joan, so I understand

. . . can I call you Joan? Well, would you like to be a messenger?"

"Messenger?" I repeated. "But they don't have lady messengers, Mr Bond, they're all men."

"They won't be, Joan, if you'll join us. You'll be a guinea pig. We're going to try ladies out. We'll get another lady as well so you won't be lonely. Your money will be twice what you are getting now."

I asked questions about what it entailed, and in the end I agreed. When I arrived back home after work I told Albert the news and he was over the moon. "Oh love, I knew you'd make something out of yourself in the end." I was sworn to secrecy, as you always were in the bank, so it's a good job I can keep my mouth shut.

The big day came. We had already been to the tailor's and had our suits made — they were good tailors, only the best for the bank.

"How do you like it?" asked the tailor.

"Too butch," came the reply. They had made us men's uniforms. "We are still women, not men."

"We don't know how to make women's suits," he said. "There wasn't any lady messenger. Sorry, I'll see what I can do about a lady's pattern." So we turned up in our trouser suits, shirts and ties. There's no wonder that the lads thought that women were going to takeover their jobs. Anyway, we took some ribbing once they were over the shock. We all used to sit for dinner in the restaurant.

"I wouldn't let my wife do this job," a little cockney at the other side of the table said.

"Then aren't I glad I'm not your wife, or we'd always be ding-donging wouldn't we?" I answered. That shut him up.

Another one said, "Well, women can't lift, can they?" Answer: "Neither can you lot by the look of it, there's four of you with bad backs. Try another one, besides, I don't lift." I didn't lift because a friend had made me a skateboard with four ball bearings on it which was very handy, and I never had any trouble moving things. Besides, my dad had taught me to do things the simplest way.

After a while on that job, I was offered a job on the tenth floor, a very good floor, and they put one of the lads with me, Ian. The messenger who should have shown us the job reported sick, so we were on our tods. He had left a short list, so we went from there.

"What are we going to do, Joan?" Ian asked. I was in charge as I had been there longer than him.

"Right, Ian, you take one set of offices, and I'll take the other." It was a doubly-large office.

"Don't panic, we've got to learn the job. Take a pencil and pad and jot down anything you learn. I'll do the same. Ask around, somebody will help you." So this is how we learned the job, and we had some fun swapping notes, but we got it sorted out in the end and we did enjoy our work.

If you wanted promotion you had to apply to another bank. I didn't bother as I liked the job I had and was in my fifties. Ian applied and was accepted. He had got married and needed more money, so he moved on. I was to have another assistant and wondered who it would be — would he be as good as Ian? I was sorry to lose him, but that's how it goes in the bank.

I had finished dishing out the mail and was having a cup of tea and a couple of biscuits when Ian's replacement came out of the lift and towards my desk. He looked like a bouncer at a night club — short, stocky, and built like an all-in wrestler. I hadn't seen him before as he was new.

"Who's in charge here?" he demanded.

"Me," I answered, looking him straight in the eye.

"A woman?" he replied.

I looked myself up and down and said, "I think so!"

I knew what had happened. The lads hadn't told him downstairs, and I bet they were waiting to see his reaction. He plonked himself down. "I've to report here for work." Then he said menacingly, "Anybody cross swords with me and they'll know about it"

"Well, let me tell you something, Sonny Jim, anybody cross swords with me and they'll know they've done it!" My hackles were up; this was not necessary. "I know exactly what's on your mind. 'Ah, a woman, and one old enough to be my mother. Well, I'm not working under a woman.' Well, I don't like chauvinist pigs, and don't give me that old chestnut that women can't do this job. I've heard it before. Well, this woman can. I've been on it for years, and I can do it with my eyes closed, right? If you don't want the job, tell them downstairs and they'll put you back on reception until another job comes up. It's no skin off my nose. Before you go, do you want a cup of tea? I've just made one."

"Yes, please," he said. "Two sugars, sorry." This offer had diffused the bomb. "I'll stay." I bet I didn't remind him of his dear old Mum, more like a Rottweiler! One thing to his credit, hc was a good worker. He needed handling right, I could see, kid gloves with iron fists in them. I noticed that with men I had to ask them to do a job, not tell them. I also asked their opinion when doing a big job, even though I didn't need their advice, and this seemed to go a long way.

One big job we had was to bring 21 filing cabinets from downstairs and swap them with the same number of old filing cabinets on our floor. We also had to change the files over. So I said, "Jack, pow-wow after dinner, we've got a big job on." So we put out heads together. "Any ideas Jack? Don't forget, the easiest way."

"How about moving them four at a time, Joan?" "Good, but we're not lifting them. I've got a square skateboard here with ball-bearing castors. I'll show you what I mean."

The personnel started at 9.00a.m. so we came in at 7.00a.m. to do the job. We eventually got it all done and the boss came in and thanked us profusely. I could see Jack's face, he was so pleased with what we'd done. His wife Jean came up from the next floor down — she had a very good job and I knew her well. She had a very good sense of humour and she asked, "What have you done with Jack He loves the job and he doesn't say a wrong word about you, Joan. He is a big head at times, you know."

"Not with me," I said. She rolled with laughter. After Jack came Craig who was a 6' 6" shirker whom I carried for two years. The less said about him, the better. Next came Ken who was the eldest at 60. I was 58, heading towards retirement, but he was older than me and didn't retire until he was 65. This was a bone of contention with him, so he would say, "It's not fair we have to work until we are 65, they should make women work the same."

"OK, Ken," I said, "I'd work until I was 65 if they would let me."

"You couldn't do it," he said, "you wouldn't have the stamina."

"Rubbish," I answered, "Mum worked until she was nearly 80."

Well, that shut him up, and I proved him wrong, as they asked me back to help them out, and I stayed until I was nearly 68. Anyway, we worked well together after I had found his Achilles heel. I asked him what job he didn't like that we did.

"Filing," was his answer.

"Well, that's easily sorted out," I said, "I'll do your filing, Ken, if you fetch the parcels of stationery upstairs and check them for me." I normally did all the stationery. Ken thought this was great, so that sorted that out. What he didn't like doing, I swapped for one of my jobs. I didn't mind what I did as I was getting well-paid for it. Well, this was mind over matter. Ken didn't mind a woman working over him, as he had been in the army and he had been a corporal but his wife was an officer. This was not supposed to happen in the

Forces. They had been married for years when he worked for me, and they were still happy together.

One day I said to him, "Can you hold the fort, Ken while I go across the road to Unit Trusts (this was the shares floor, where they bought and sold shares)?"

"Have you bought some shares, Joan?"

"Yes, Ken, I bought them when I started here. As I am retiring soon, I'm going to sell them. I'll just go across and see how much I've got to come. Mind you, I've had some good dividends off them."

So I trotted across the road, went to the counter, and asked for Hazel who was a manager. They nearly all knew me, as I had been on security at both sides of the road. Hazel was only too glad to oblige. She had a piece of paper in her hand, but I wasn't expecting much because I'd had good dividends. However, some of them were accumulators, and if you left your dividends in, you got more money.

"Close your eyes Joan," Hazel said, so I did. "Now open them, I think you've hit the jackpot" So I opened my eyes and looked.

"Oh, Hazel!" is all I could say. There it was, £9,000 for my £2,000, so I had made £7,000. It took me a few minutes to recover. Don't forget, this was about 1982 when money was money. I didn't know anything about shares then, but I vowed that I would by the time that I had finished. I was a glutton for learning. I wanted to know what made them tick. I always knew that they could go down as well as up, but I wanted to know the pitfalls.

"What's up, Joan?" Ken asked when I got back. "You don't look very well, I'll make you a cup of tea." Now that was something, coming from Ken, as I always made the tea.

"No, Ken," I said, "I'm not ill, I'm in shock. Take a gander at that, then you have a cup of tea." So he looked, and I hoped that he wouldn't have a funny turn. He couldn't believe his eyes.

"I think I'll get some shares of my own," he said. "Be careful, Ken," I warned, "It's not as easy as that. Get financial advice first. Here's a fiver, Ken, get yourself a couple of pints."

Well, this lasted all week because he loved a pint with his dinner. After dinner he would do anything for me, he was like a pussycat.

Earlier on I mentioned that when I married Albert and I changed my name from Jackson to Belk, I couldn't do anything wrong, my luck had changed. I was like Midas, everything I touched turned to gold, and it continued. I went home elated.

"Albert?"

"Yes," he replied, "What have you been doing now?"

"Well, these are those shares I bought," I answered, "I've made a bit of money — I've sold them."

"Oh, how much?" he asked.

"I've made £7,000, and with the original £2,000 it makes £9,000."

"Am I hearing properly?" he asked.

"Yes, love, and I have an idea." The electric light had lit up in the top of my head again.

112

"I must give you credit, love," Albert said, "You are getting quicker. Go on, let's hear it"

"We could invest it in the house — we could get the corporation to value the house and we could buy it, and this would save us over £20 per week."

"Good idea, love, good idea."

So we had the house valued. It's a lovely house on a nice estate — private, with a large garden that had a hedge all round it, nice neighbours, and no-one over-looking. As we had been in it for over 20 years we got it for £8,000. We couldn't believe it, so we bought it, and it turned out to be a good investment, didn't it?

Before I retired, there was a terrible tragedy at the bank. One day, at about ten minutes before four, I'd just finished my last duty emptying all the waste paper bins into a black bag, and I was walking back to my desk along the corridor when one of the young managers passed me. He was always pleasant, and we always had a little laugh about something, but he didn't say anything this time, so I asked, "Aren't we talking today then?" He looked at me and said, "Sorry, Joan, I didn't see you" and he went on. I thought he looked a bit stressed because he was smoking a cigarette quickly and his hair looked a bit untidy. I went back to my desk and got ready for going home after I had put away everything that I was using. I put my coat on, picked my bag up, went down in the lift, and left, saying goodnight to the lads on the doors.

I didn't know a thing until I went into work the next morning — there was one messenger on the desk, but all the rest had buckets of water and brushes and were scrubbing away. So I said, "They haven't got you doing that job now, have they?" Nobody laughed. I thought it was strange as we were always joking, so they told me what had happened, and my blood ran cold. As I came out of the door the day before, at just after four o'clock, Mr B from our floor had gone up to the twelfth floor and thrown himself out of the window. It had made a terrible mess outside.

I put the kettle on and made us a cup of tea with some sugar in. All the energy had gone out of the building — everyone was in shock, and the temperature of the building had gone down several degrees. I am sensitive and feel things. Every time I went down the corridor I shivered when I passed the spot where I had seen him, poor man. I didn't hear anything when I went home as I'm partly deaf and can hardly hear anything from behind, thank goodness. I'd have been shocked to have seen it. Dennis in the print room on the ninth floor was looking out at the weather when the body passed the window — he wasn't very well for weeks after that. Eventually the feeling went and we got back to normal.

I was creeping nearer retirement, and I wasn't looking forward to it — I wasn't ready for it. When it came we had a lovely party, and they had a collection which paid for me to learn drawing at the London College of Art via correspondence. This would save me from getting bored, and I was so grateful. At last I had retired. So I thought.

Two weeks later I had a phone call from the bank. Could I go and help them out, as they were very busy?

So that's what I did. One of the shortest retirements on record, I should think. Mind you, I was full time for three months, then part-time, which I was pleased about, because I wanted to ease myself into retirement. My boss was very nice.

"Come what hours you like, Joan, and finish when you've had enough."

So I did seven years altogether, but I enjoyed every minute. Guess where they put me? The Unit Trust floor, which was the share floor. Oh boy, it was like having a long birthday. So on Monday morning I went to Courtwood House for nine o'clock — that was the small building, across from the big clearing department from where I had retired. I had worked there on security in reception when I had just been made a messenger, so I knew practically all the people in the building. It reminded me, when I walked in, of the day that the top manager came down the stairs with Nancy, his secretary.

"We are just going across to the reproduction room, Joan," he said.

I replied simply, "Oh yes, Mr Cole."

He looked at me and we all laughed — he got the message, he had meant the reprographic room!

"Well, Joan, I shall have to rephrase that, won't I?" His secretary came down later and told me that they had had a good laugh about it.

"But I only said a few words," I said.

"Yes, but it was how you said them, Joan," she answered.

So I went to the floor I was going to work on. Robert, one of the managers, came up to me and said, "Hello Joan, what are you doing here?"

"Come to help you out, Robert," I replied.

"Good, Joan, we could do with your help, follow me." So we found a desk that was vacant and I started. I was putting leaflets in envelopes, hundreds of them. I finished that lot and went for something else to do.

"You are fast, Joan, I didn't think that you would do them as quickly as that," Robert said.

"I used to be on piecework at one of the places I worked at before," I told him. The boss came up and thanked me.

"Joan, just look around for jobs and do what you want, you don't need any supervision." He knew me when I had been a messenger, and we never needed supervision then.

The next thing that my eyes clapped on was the filing — what a mess, papers were strewn on top of the filing cabinets, and some had slid down the back. So I fetched ten empty boxes from the box room — they were boxes that had had computer paper in them, so they were being thrown away. I filed the papers in these boxes in the Trusts section, against an empty wall. After I had done that, I was asked, "Joan, have you seen any files floating about?"

"Yes, Mr Sawyer, they're there in those boxes against the wall, I've got to sort them into numbers yet."

He looked as if he was going to kiss me. "Good job done, Joan — it takes about an hour to find what you want, and we are always in a hurry." Off he went with a box and a few minutes later, as pleased as Punch, he brought it back. I didn't know then, but this was the start of what became a filing room later on.

A man came to work with me on leaflets as we had a promotion on, and there were tens of thousands of them. He was Griff, and he had been a manager in one of the banks in the city. They were closing his branch down, so I thought he had taken early retirement as he was in his early forties. Anyway, we got on all right, and we finished up working for about six years together.

After about twelve months at Courtwood House, we moved to another bank, further down in the city as our offices weren't big enough. Our new premises were very nice with plenty of room and we were very pleased with them. We had a long double office, and a smaller mail office where we did all the mail and parcels. Then I had a small office for the files — it had a desk and a chair, and lovely large windows. There were three of us — David, an ex-messenger, Griff and myself, and we were very busy. Business was booming.

One day I was filling in a form for some shares when Griff asked, "Are you buying some shares, Joan?"

"Yes," I replied, "I often buy some."

"What are you buying?"

"High Street, Griff. It's a new issue that has come out, they're cheap just now, but they'll probably go up after a while."

"I think I'll get some myself," Griff said.

So I tried to tell him not to follow what I was buying, as it was instinct with me after studying shares. Well, it

117

didn't make any difference, and Griff followed me for about six years.

Did we do well? Every day Griff and I looked at how our shares were doing — we studied *The Financial Times*, a monthly book on shares, and anything I could glean from the share managers, as they knew me from when I had been a messenger. It became our hobby and we enjoyed the excitement — we never became bored. At night when Albert and I were relaxing, we would talk about what we had done with our shares. We did cut some capers at times, but we never lost any money, and Albert would laugh about things and back me every inch of the way.

At night I studied all that was happening in the papers, then the next day I discussed with Griff what I had got in mind and sometimes we would then buy more shares. This went on for about three years without losing any money. Then one day I had this strange feeling, which I get at times.

"Albert, I'm going to sell all my shares," at which Albert looked surprised, and asked, "What's brought this on? You are doing so well."

"I think the bubble's going to burst — I've been watching the Americans and they seem to be going over the top. Anyway, I've done well with them, so I'm not chancing it" So, next day I told Griff, and he said he would sell his as well. It got around that I had sold my shares, and others in the same frame of mind did the same. Neville, the under-manager, sold his, but Robert, the other one, had gone on holiday — Neville rang Robert to see if he wanted to sell his, but Robert thought things would recover. This was August 1987, and the bubble did burst In the meantime I had bought Granny Bonds at 7.5% fixed rate for five years — was I glad! My premonitions, or funny feelings, as Albert used to say, paid off that time. Shares went right through the floor and the atmosphere in the office became terrible as there was no trading — they all sat there chewing their pencils, looking very confused. It was the same freezing feeling as when the tragedy had happened a few years earlier — the terrible feeling of shock, very frightening. We had to be content with reading about shares and watching their slow progress, and we carried on like this for another couple of years.

When I left the shop I invested part of the money I got in Victorian gold sovereigns which were in very good condition and cost £15 each. Instead of drawing our savings out of the bank, I had another idea. I remembered the sovereigns in a little box upstairs, and after telling Albert what I was going to do, he said, "You know what you're doing, love." Famous last words. So off I trotted to the jewellers.

"Do you buy gold coins?" I asked.

"Yes, I'll just take them in the back to the manager;" Back he came. "I'm sorry, Mrs Belk, but gold has gone down this week, they're only paying £46 each."

"Oh dear," I said, "but I'll have to sell them as I need the money." I couldn't believe my luck. I had 13 which I had bought at £15 each, so that was £598 in my hand. I don't know about being unlucky, it wasn't for me. "Yabbadabbadoo," I could have shouted, but it wasn't very lady-like in town.

Then one day when I was off from the bank and the manager was on a six-week course, Griff rang me up to tell me that all pensioners and temps had finished. When I went to work he told me what had happened. Head Office had sent a keen career-ladder-climbing young woman to reorganise the office, so she did — she picked the pensioners, the most hard-working and vulnerable, to let go. So I went to see her and gave her both barrels — I was mad, how dare she tell someone else to tell me that I had finished. She should have had more respect for people, if she knew what that meant, and should have told me to my face. She probably didn't like older people because they had more experience than herself. Anyway, she looked right sheepish when I left.

The next day Mr Sawyer called me into his office and apologised, saying that that shouldn't have happened. He thanked me for the help I had given him over the years. I had been with them for six years, and no-one had supervised me all that time as I had got on with any job that wanted doing. He gave me a letter of thanks as well. "I've got a bit of good news for you Joan," he said, "you haven't finished work yet. I've managed to get you and Griff a part-time job downstairs on probate, doing the same work. I'm loathe to part with you both. Go and look at the job, Joan, and tell me if you want it"

I thanked him very much for being a good boss, and sent Griff in. Later we went to see what the job entailed, accepted it, and went back to tell Mr Sawyer, who was very pleased. The others in the office were sorry to see us go as they had to do their own mail and filing, and they didn't like that as it got in such a mess after a while.

David wasn't with us then, he had managed to get a better job. A few months earlier we had been talking at break time and I said, "David, are you going to be in this job until you retire? Don't you ever think of promotion?"

"I do, Joan, but what can I do — I couldn't get a better job here, could I?"

"Yes, you could, if you tried. You're a good organizer." He perked up at this. "Next time the vacancies form comes round, have a look and apply if it suits you, you don't know what might happen." So he did, and managed to get a job in our block of offices on stationery, with about four men under him whom he knew well as they were all ex-messengers.

I gave David one bit of advice when he left — never to let them dangle a carrot in his face, always study the job well first, and if he felt any doubt, don't take it. I had seen this many times — the money was the draw, then the job was too much for them, and then they had stress. About three years later Albert and I met David in the town. David told Albert how glad he was to see me, as he wanted to thank me personally, because he had applied for a better job and got it. He was going to work in Bristol. He said he would always remember the carrot bit; and when he left, Albert smiled at me and said, "Oh yes." He understood what David had said. I miss those days.

Before concluding this chapter I must record that during my early years at the bank Pauline met Tony — it would have been in about 1980. Tony had three children, Nicola, Lee and Zoë, and after several years Pauline and Tony decided to get married. Like me, she has found happiness second time around, for which I'm delighted.

Retirement

I finished work in 1992, as there was no more work for us to do on the Probate floor. I had had a good run for my money, so I couldn't grumble as I was now 68. As usual, I was only at home for a few weeks when one of my work colleagues rang up and asked if I wanted a job on the mail and filing.

"Iris, did you tell them that I'm heading for 70?" "Yes, of course. I told them that you had just finished at the bank after nearly 17 years, and you were very conscientious." She explained that we would be freelance and wouldn't have any holiday money, so they could stop us when they wanted to.

I also had an excellent reference from the bank. The job was mine if I wanted it, but I turned it down, as I thought that it was time I retired. Iris understood, as after all I had been working for 53 years with only a few short breaks.

However, I still couldn't settle at home, so I went for painting lessons at college for four years, then Yoga and meditation, and keep-fit lessons.

Finally, at 75 I started computer classes at college, finishing at the age of 78, when I received my certificate for word-processing. Now I am writing my book. I wonder what else is round the corner?

Every year I took Mum on holiday. Albert didn't go, as like my dad he didn't like holidays. Our favourite holidays were going to London for five days. Then we would hop over to Paris for five days, then back to London, or we'd go to Torquay. The last time Mum and I went she was in her 80s, and she was a good walker so we used to walk miles. Mind you, she didn't stop work until she was 80, helping in a public house. When asked her age she was always 69!

Mum lived near us for years and we looked after her. All of a sudden she decided to live near my two brothers at Rotherham, and she managed to get a second floor flat with a garden. Mum didn't tell me there was a garden. She was 85 by now, but very lively, and everybody liked her because she had charisma and a mind of her own. She used to say, "Don't tie me down, I'm a free spirit." She could draw men to her, and they would do anything for her.

One day Pauline and I went to see Mum, and she said to us, "Girls, I've clicked." That meant that she had made a conquest, and she introduced us to Bert over the railings on the balcony. You could tell that they liked one another from the beginning. He was good-looking and very pleasant with a lovely smile, and he had been a sailor when he was younger — you could tell, because he was spotlessly clean. The only thing was that he was 25 years younger than Mum, but it didn't mean a thing to them, and they were firm friends for seven years. Every morning he would have her breakfast ready and then she would stay until dinner time, when they would have a walk around and do some shopping. They would have their tea, watch television, and at bedtime he would take her to her flat and make sure that she was safe and sound.

Mum was so lucky to have someone like that. I used to take them a fresh turkey or chicken sandwich with a blackcurrant tart on Saturday when Albert went to the organ shop where his friend was the manager — he would sit there for hours talking to the customers, he really enjoyed it.

Then one day, when Mum was 92, she collapsed and had to go into hospital. Bert, at 70, was practically blind; I was 70, and Albert was 72 with Angina. I was getting run down and couldn't manage looking after Mum anymore, as she wouldn't come to live with us or with my brother John and his wife Floss. Floss knew an ex-hospital sister who ran a small residential home, an old Victorian rectory with only ten people in it. Mum was all right there for about six years.

With the help of a friend and his car, Bert visited Mum at the residential home, but it had been so long that she had forgotten his name. However, it didn't upset him, so long as he'd been to visit her. All my Mum could say to me was, "Two lovely young men came to see me. I knew one of them, but I didn't know his name." Ironic, isn't it? Life is like that. Mum died in 1995 at the age of 98.

During the time that Mum was in the home, I'd visited Bert every week and taken him the sandwiches as usual. Sometimes I would phone him on a Sunday, and once he called me, saying "I'm coming out of hospital tomorrow, Joan." I didn't know that he had been in; apparently they had thought that he was going to have a heart attack. "I'll come and see you tomorrow Bert," I said.

"Ok Joan, till tomorrow," he replied. But the next morning his brother Bill rang me. "Joan, I'm sorry love, but we've lost our Bert. He died of a heart attack during the night." I was stunned, and Albert sat me down and gave me a drop of whiskey and ginger ale. "Poor Bert," he said, "he's been such a good friend to you and your mum." I wept because Bert had been a loner and his family had not bothered about him and he had no other friends. Bert died only a fortnight after Mum. The solicitor asked for myself and Bert's brother to go to his office as we were executors of his will.

"Before I start," he said, "Bert left a message before he died. He thanks you, Mrs Belk, for being a good friend, one of the best, and he has left you £4,000."

I nearly collapsed with shock, and questioned whether I could benefit as an executor, but the solicitor said that I could, adding that it was a nice compliment. When I arrived home I told Albert, and he was as surprised as I was. He asked me what I was going to spend it on. We had just ordered a conservatory for the back of the house, and as I didn't want to spend Bert's money on any old rubbish, we agreed to pay for the conservatory with it and dedicate it to Bert. I had kept in touch with Bert and kept my eye on him because he had looked after Mum, and I was so grateful to him that I tried to repay him — yet he was so grateful to me that he was trying to repay me. That was lovely.

Albert's hobby was playing the organ. He was self-taught, and could play anything. While he played the organ with his earphones on, I used to work on my computer, and that is how we used to pass some of our time together.

It was February 17th 2001 — Albert and I had had two lovely days together. Not that we hadn't been happy before, we were, but these were two special days. When we went to bed that Sunday we were in good spirits. I should have known, I'd seen it happen many times before with other people. We had been talking about what would happen if one of us died and left the other on their own, and we had been very straightforward with one another.

"Joan, I haven't long to go now," Albert said.

"Oh, don't say that, love," I replied.

"We've got to be sensible about things like this. I don't want you grieving a long time as some do, love, I want you to be strong and to look after yourself. If you go on crying and crying you'll make yourself ill, and then our Pauline will have to look after you, and we don't want that, do we? Don't forget, love, that we have had 38 lovely years. I'm living on borrowed time, I'm 78 you know, and if your number's up, nobody can stop it. I shall be floating about somewhere, and if you hear 'Yabbadabbadoo', you know that I'm somewhere near."

This was our secret password which we had used for years. If he looked at a picture and liked it, Albert would say, "Yabbadabbadoo, love?" and I would answer back the same, and then we would have a good laugh.

The next day I was sat up in bed for an hour to keep Albert company. Then I got up, fed the cat, and put the heating on to warm the house for when Albert got up. However, that morning he sat up and said, "Joan love, I feel ill." I phoned the ambulance, instead of wasting time calling the doctor, as Albert had had three heart attacks and so time was of the essence. I knew that I could not save him as he looked at me and said, "Joan, love, this is it, this is it," and I answered, "Oh no, my little love."

"I can't breathe, it's getting worse."

I was trying to keep his head up as I had been instructed to do by the nurse over the phone. The ambulance men rushed upstairs for him, I kissed his forehead, and in one minute they had taken him down to the ambulance but they wouldn't let me in. I had to wait while they tried to resuscitate him, but I knew that this would be the last time I would see Albert alive. His number had come up, and I knew that he had died.

I could not cry and my feelings had gone dead. In hospital the nurse came in and before she had time to say anything, I said, "I know my husband's gone." She looked at me, puzzled, and then asked me where my daughter was. Pauline was working only a few minutes from the hospital, so they said that they would fetch her as I was in shock. I tried to explain that I wasn't, and asked them to break it to Pauline gently. A bit later when they brought her in she was almost hysterical, and I calmed her down.

"Pauline," I said, "I knew Albert was going to die. He told me, and we've got to be brave. I'm sure he's watching over us." She calmed down, and we went to the cafe and had a cup of tea and talked it over without any hysterics. We at last accepted the inevitable. I loved Albert very much for everything he stood for.

Life after Albert

I met Doreen Hill, my closest friend, at painting lessons when Albert was still alive. How we laughed when we started, as we didn't know one end of the paintbrush from another. Fourteen years ago Doreen was just beginning to recover from ME, and it takes years to get over it. We had some fun painting. One day the tutor said, "Paint a picture of your own; let's see if you can do it." So I painted a picture that night, and was very pleased with it. I asked Albert what he thought, and he said, "You've done well, love, you're a learner." I was proud of it, and when Doreen and I were showing each other our pictures the next day, the teacher walked in. We thought that he must have got out of bed on the wrong side, as he asked us what they were supposed to be.

"Pictures," we said.

"You could have fooled me," he replied.

Now I don't like slow timers. Looking at mine, he asked what it was, and I asked him what it looked like. "Poppies in a field?"

"Right," I answered. If he had said an elephant stood on its head, I would have agreed. I was fed up with him.. We started laughing, and it took us some time to settle down. Another time he advised us to bring a receptacle to put plenty of water in. The next session he looked at us and said, "I didn't mean as big as that," looking down at our plastic jars. I can't remember which one of us said, "Well, we could have brought a bucket," but we laughed again. I don't think we liked him much, even though it was costing a lot.

Anyway, the next time I met Doreen at the art class, we were pleased to see one another, and we became good friends. Albert always called her "My good friend Doreen". It's nice to have a good friend and I really appreciate it. In the end we painted some good pictures and had some in an exhibition in a city theatre.

My grandson Mark comes to see me every Tuesday or Wednesday. We get on like a house on fire, and have a lot in common, such as The Beatles and old British films. He is a film buff, and has recorded about 400, most of which I have seen before. If he asks me who stars in them, I can tell him most names, which he then checks in his film book — it's a kind of game between us which we enjoy playing. Mark was married briefly and had two children, Haley and Darryl, whom he loves dearly.

Mark, now 37, was born when The Beatles were famous. When he was small he used to enjoy me playing their records from the Apple Studios, and though they are now valuable, Mark wouldn't part with them. Recently Mark took me to Liverpool to see where The Beatles came from. We had a lovely time going to The Cavern, and other places. I told him about

131

the time when I met Paul McCartney in London. I had taken my mother, his Great-Grandma, there, and we were walking along looking for the Victoria and Albert Museum. We saw a young man looking over the railings on a crossroad, watching the traffic go by, and he asked us if we were on holiday. We told him we were from Sheffield for a week, that we loved London, and after a short chat we thanked him and crossed the road. As we turned round he waved at us and was laughing. I tried to remember where I had seen him before. I tapped my forehead and said, "Oh! It's Paul McCartney Mum, you know, one of The Beatles!" He pointed to himself, mimed 'yes', and we all laughed. He waved goodbye.

A strange thing happened the other week. I had three phone calls, all from the same voice, and he would mumble that he had the wrong number and then put the phone down. When my grandson, Mark, came back from work for a cup of tea and a chat, I told him about the calls. I wondered if they were "sizing the joint up", as the Americans say.

"Well, Miss Marple," joked Mark, "If he can get into your house, then he's a good one, because it's like Fort Knox — six doors with safety locks, a good alarm, every door bolted. If they managed to get out of one room into another it would be a miracle." (Although my next-door neighbour can get in when there is an emergency.) Anyway, a day or two later, I walked down the garden to see if everything was all right. I backtracked to the greenhouse, where I realized my arrangement of cacti in a very large earthenware pot, which I couldn't even lift as it was so heavy, was missing. It had one very large cactus at the back that was just flowering with large yellow flowers, and a variety of others around the edge. I had had the pot for 15 years. There were also two or three smaller pots, but they had been left, so the burglars knew what they were after.

I phoned my daughter, Pauline, and told her about the theft. She couldn't believe it, as the pot was so large — she thought it would be dicing with death to steal it! I started laughing, and she observed how I always see the funny side of things.

"Well," I said, "it is funny if you think about it. I have been trying to get rid of it, because I used to get those needles in my hands every time I watered it or fed it. It was never grateful, and I wanted to get rid of it. It must be worth about £50 to anyone who collected cacti, so whoever stole it has done me a favour. The only thing is the two young cacti must miss their mother, I wish they had stolen them as well."

"Mother, you and your jokes," said Pauline.

I had been made the new chairperson of the Over-Fifties Cub. One day I had to announce the speaker, so I stood up and said, "Attention, everybody." No response. So I knocked on the table with my glasses case, which got attention. "The speaker tonight is George [about my age, in his 70s]. He is going to give us a talk on using the trampoline and how to swing from the chandeliers." That woke them up, and I said, after a second or two, "Oh, sorry, George, I've got the wrong page. With George it's games, give him a big hand!" The session got off to a good start, we laughed and laughed. I do get the devil in me sometimes, when people look a bit sombre!

At Easter time 2001, Pauline and Tony hired a six-berth caravan with two friends, and they took me with them. I had just lost Albert three months earlier, but this trip helped me a lot with my bereavement, and I enjoyed it very much. I had been a bit apprehensive at first — how were five adults going to manage in a caravan, and would we be in each other's way? However, I was pleasantly surprised, as the caravan was large with plenty of room inside, and everything you need was supplied. In addition, the buses, shops and seafront were all nearby.

Meanwhile I received a letter from the tax office, which had done terrible things to my tax code, and they told me that now I was a widow I had tax to pay on Albert's pension and savings etc. I went to the building society and asked them what I had to do, and they asked me to fill in a form so that I could pay tax on all my savings. When I was told I only got one percent interest on my current account, I couldn't believe it — tax you up to the hilt, lower your interest on everything, then take your house if you have to move into a private residential home where they charge about £450 per week or more. "Oh no they don't," I thought, so I slept on it, as I always do, and I came to the conclusion that there was no point in saving when it's taken off you, while other people just enter the country and get what ever they want.

At about the end of September, I got the family together for a "pow-wow" — Pauline, Tony, Mark and myself. I started talking.

"If I bought you a fully-equipped caravan and paid the ground rent for the first year, could you manage after that?" They had to make a cup of tea to let it sink in. I continued: "First of all it will be in Pauline's and Tony's names, but Mark and I can use it when it's empty. Does everyone agree?" They did, and we drank our tea in silence.

We now had to find a suitable caravan, so we looked at the papers to see what there was. I was prepared to buy a new one, but one day, shortly after, Pauline telephoned me to say that she thought she had found one that matched our requirements, but it was second-hand. I didn't think that it would do, but agreed to go and see it so as not to disappoint Pauline. She went to the owner's house for the keys, and said that they were a lovely couple — a retired ex-miner and his wife who had had a heart attack, so that they wouldn't need the caravan anymore. They also needed the money badly, in cash.

So we went to see the caravan on a cold but sunny day. There were five of us in Dennis's car, and we soon found the caravan on a newish site. It was in excellent condition on the outside, but when we went inside we all gasped — the place was so immaculate. Pauline made us a cup of tea, and we sat mesmerised — we couldn't believe our eyes. We looked in cupboard doors, went into the built-in wardrobes in the bedroom, where there was a pine king-size bed with a lovely duvet on, looked at the shower and toilet, the dining-area with table, gas-fire and seats that converted into beds at night-time, the kitchen with stainless-steel oven, fridge and cupboards and even a vacuum cleaner — everything was spotless and complete. The seating had all been re-upholstered, and there was a covering on the walls that you could easily wash down. The ceiling was done in the same material, only lighter in colour, with round lights fitted. There was shag-pile carpet on the floor, and blue curtains and white nets on the windows. We were stunned, so we had another cup of tea and the salmon sandwiches that I had made, and set off home as it would soon get dark.

Pauline and Tony went to the owners' house and agreed that we would buy the caravan. They showed the papers to prove that they owned it; they were very honest. They then sent their two grown-up grandsons to close down the caravan and pack everything away for the winter. They were very pleased when we paid the money to them, as they had been expecting us to try and knock the price down, but we didn't, as it was worth every penny — in fact, more. I had invested my money in happiness, that's what I thought about it. When we went at the start of the season, we had the happy feeling that we were going to enjoy ourselves, as the caravan was so comfortable. We have had it now for two seasons, and are looking forward to the next. Everyone who has been in it has enjoyed themselves.

One day on holiday, we were walking down a street and Pauline said, "Mum, I bet Albert would have loved our caravan, don't you?"

I replied, "Yes, he would, but I thought he would have got in touch with me somehow. He said I would hear or see 'Yabbadabbadoo', and I haven't yet, and it's been over two and a half years."

"Mother, look over the road. How much proof do you want?"

We all looked and couldn't believe our eyes.

There, over the shop, was the name "Yabbadabbadoo", and I said back, "Yabbadabbadoo, love." We laughed and laughed, it made our day, and I just remembered to get my camera out and take a couple of photos. When I look up at Albert's photo, he seems to smile at me and say, "That was a good idea, love. Yabbadabbadoo, love."

"Yabbadabbadoo Albert."

Postscript

Well, I realize now as I am getting older that I've had a varied life, and I have lots to be thankful for. I was an introvert, and it was like coming through a tunnel when I became an extrovert. Studying mind over matter helped me achieve this, so that I was not frightened of anything or anybody. I would have been a beaten wife if I had let it carry on. I have seen both sides of the coin. I have worked in filthy jobs with poor pay, and then I've known plenty of money; I've had a poor marriage and a good one; I have been in the Air Force, which I wouldn't have missed for the world, and I have been in business buying and selling anything. I saved Albert's life by massaging his heart vigorously when he had his first heart attack, and I helped him through 20 years of Angina and three more heart attacks — he was never any trouble.

I've had two near-death experiences, one going down a tunnel and dragging myself back. I have levitated to the ceiling twice — I could have gone out of the window to explore, but as I was enjoying myself, I didn't go any further, in case the silver cord broke, and so I landed back in bed with Albert — he was thrilled to bits when I told him, because he understood these things. I do meditation and I used to do Yoga. I have worked at a large clearing bank, miles apart from buffing at a steel works, but I loved doing both jobs. All of these I call achievements, and I hope the writing of this book is another one to add to the list.

Living on Tick

Hazel Wheeler

"Part of our war effort at Central Stores must surely have been in helping to keep people's spirits up. Even in wartime there has to be humour or we'd all be dead. Not from bullets but from sheer monotony."

The corner shop in the 1920s and '30s was much more than just a place to buy the groceries. It was a meeting place where familiar faces, on both sides of the counter, swapped stories and helped each other out. People bought groceries daily, so visits to the shop were a frequent occurrence and when times were hard it was common for a customer to ask for, and usually get, goods "on tick".

Hazel Wheeler grew up in her father's shop in Deighton near Huddersfield and recalls her memories of those times. She remembers the people, the goods they sold in the shop and a way of life that has now vanished.

ISBN 0-7531-9362-0 (hb)
ISBN 0-7531-9363-9 (pb)

The Way We Were

Toni Savage

"Everything had two alternatives for us. The season was either summer or winter. The days were either good or bad. There was out or in. Out was most of the time."

An only child, Toni Savage was evacuated from London in September 1939. She was to spend over four years in the Surrey countryside, living in a country mansion with seven other children, under the watchful eyes of Mrs Parrot, Miss Bailey and the governess Mrs Samuel.

Although her life as an evacuee was often one of fun and laughter, full of new friends and the wonders of childhood, it was also lived in the shadow of the war, with both bombs and soldiers a common sight.

ISBN 0-7531-9344-2 (hb)
ISBN 0-7531-9345-0 (pb)